200 MORE SLOW COOKER RECIPES

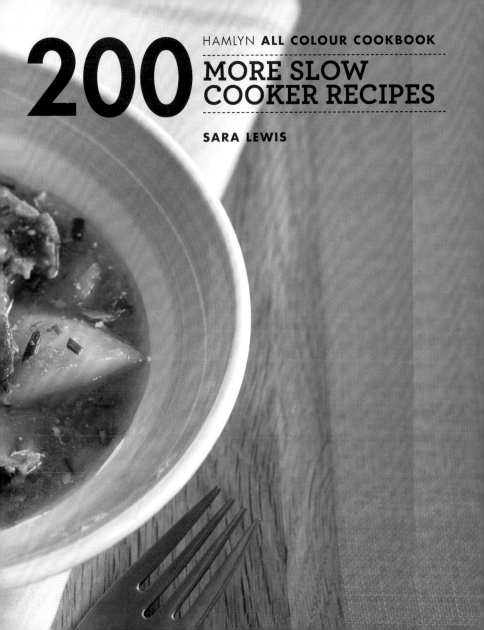

HAMLYN **ALL COLOUR COOKBOOK**

200
MORE SLOW
COOKER RECIPES

SARA LEWIS

An Hachette UK Company
www.hachette.co.uk

First published in Great Britain in 2011 by Hamlyn,
a division of Octopus Publishing Group Ltd
Carmelite House, 50 Victoria Embankment
London EC4Y 0DZ
www.octopusbooks.co.uk

This edition published in 2016

ISBN 978-0-600-63333-4

A CIP catalogue record for this book is available from the British
Library

Printed and bound in China

10 9 8 7 6 5 4 3 2 1

Standard level spoon measurement are used in all recipes.
1 tablespoon = one 15 ml spoon
1 teaspoon = one 5 ml spoon

Both imperial and metric measures have been given in all
recipes. Use one set of measurements only and not a mixture
of both.

Eggs should be medium unless otherwise stated. The
Department of Health advises that eggs should not be
consumed raw. This book contains dishes made with raw or
lightly cooked eggs. It is prudent for more vulnerable people
such as pregnant and nursing mothers, invalids, the elderly,
babies and young children to avoid uncooked or lightly cooked
dishes made with eggs. Once prepared these dishes should
be kept refrigerated and used promptly.

Fresh herbs should be used unless otherwise stated.

A few recipes contain nuts and nut derivatives. Anyone with
a known nut allergy must avoid these.

Read your slow cooker manual before you begin and preheat
the slow cooker if required according to the manufacturer's
instructions. Slow cookers vary slightly from manufacturer to
manufacturer, so do check recipe timings against manufacturer's
directions for a recipe using the same ingredients.

All recipes for this book were tested in oval-shaped slow cookers
with a working capacity of 2.5 litres (4 pints) and total capacity of
3.5 litres (6 pints) using metric measurements. Where the slow
cooker recipe is finished off under the grill, hold the pot with
teacloths to remove it from the machine housing.

contents

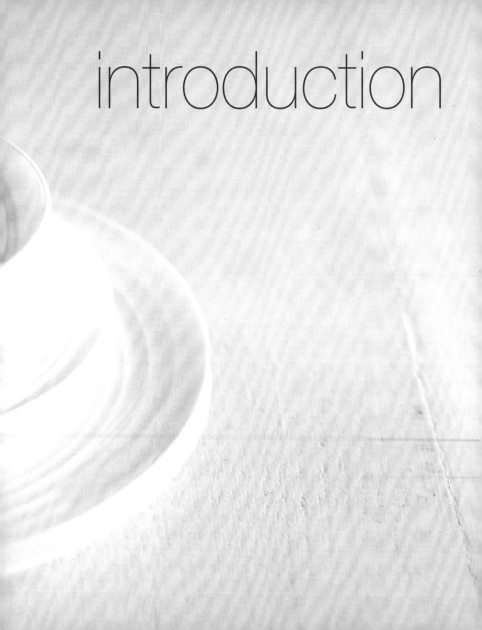

introduction

introduction

It might seem a contradiction in terms but if you are short of time and cash a slow cooker could be the answer. Grabbing a cook-chill meal from the supermarket as you struggle to get home is not relaxing or cheap, especially when feeding a family. Adjusting the way you cook may solve the problem – trying to fit everything in at the end of the day when everyone is tired is not always the best solution.

Making supper first thing may sound odd, but why not come back and get supper on after dropping the kids at school in the morning or add things to the slow cooker pot before you even get dressed in your smart work clothes? Then, when you walk in the door later in the day, what could be more welcoming than the lovely aroma of supper ready and waiting. Or, if you feel you wouldn't be organized enough for this, get the slow cooker bubbling away on a Saturday morning so that you are free to do all those things you

want to – enjoy time with the family, get on with a DIY or gardening project, or spend a few hours at the gym.

Throughout this book there are recipes for all kind of occasions – from food to share with friends to everyday basics, warming soups for lunch to cheap, filling end-of-the-month suppers. While everyone knows that a slow cooker is great for cooking meaty casseroles, there are also light, fresh-tasting fish dishes or great recipes for those who would rather have a veggie option and even puddings, too, for those days when you need spoiling. There are recipes for hot punches and preserves -- perhaps not the kind of slow cooker recipes that automatically spring to mind.

choosing a slow cooker

Slow cookers come in a range of sizes and shapes but the most versatile must be the mid-sized, oval-shaped slow cooker – it is large enough to pot roast a chicken or half shoulder of lamb, to make a meaty casserole or chilli for four, a soup for six or a steamed pud, or four individual puds, for a weekend treat. When shopping, look for one that has a total capacity of 3.5 litres (6 pints) and a working capacity of 2.5 litres (4 pints). All the recipes in this book have been tested in a slow cooker this size, but if you choose to buy a bigger or smaller cooker, simply halve the

ingredients or add half as much again where appropriate.

It is easy to get carried away and buy a large slow cooker on special offer. These may seem good value, but a slow cooker really needs to be half-full with food to work well, so if there are only four in your family do you really want to be cooking casseroles for six each time you use your slow cooker?

Recipes cooked in a pudding basin, individual dishes or a soufflé-style dish can be cooked in the larger slow cooker in just the same way as the mid-sized slow cooker – there will just be more room for water around the dishes.

If you are a couple rather than a family you may prefer to buy the mid-sized slow cooker and freeze the extra two portions for another night. Also look out for the smaller two-portion-sized slow cookers with a maximum capacity of 1.5 litres (2½ pints) and a working capacity of 1 litre (1¾ pints).

Some of the more expensive models have slow cooker pots that can also be used on the hob to fry foods first, but if you already have a good frying pan this is not an essential requirement.

Choose a slow cooker with high and low settings and an indicator light so that you can see at a glance if the slow cooker is on before you leave the house. Nothing is more frustrating than coming home to find you forgot to turn the slow cooker on after all! Check the lid of the slow cooker, too, when buying – the best models have a lid without a steam vent.

what can I cook in it?

A slow cooker is surprisingly versatile. It is well known that it cooks savoury casseroles well, but it is also great for steamed puds. Unlike simmering a basin in a steamer, where you need to regularly check the water levels in the bottom of the pan, a slow cooker is very unlikely to boil dry, so you can put the pudding on to cook and then practically forget about it. If cooking a large Sunday lunch or a big Christmas dinner it also means that you can free up an extra ring on the hob, which can be invaluable. As with all slow cooker recipes, if you get a little delayed the pudding will not spoil. However old fashioned steamed puddings may be, they are very often made with store-cupboard ingredients meaning one can be rustled up without a special shopping trip or at great expense.

9

For something a little lighter, try a warm chocolate mousse pud or delicate baked custard, crème brûlée or crème caramel pudding, even a baked cheesecake. Baked apples are very successful, as are fresh and fruity compotes, which are delicious with yogurt or ice cream.

Using the slow cooker as a water bath also means that you can bake savoury dishes, too, such as a baked egg tortilla or frittata. Pâtés and terrines can also be made, while slow-cooked duck rillettes – a French version of potted meat – are particularly successful, cooked directly in the slow cooker pot.

Although meaty casseroles are great, fish recipes also work very well. The gentle heat means that the fish stays moist and doesn't break into pieces during cooking. Try mackerel, trout, a large piece of salmon or individual portions. Shellfish can be added, but do so at the end of cooking and make sure that prawns, squid or mussels are thoroughly defrosted if frozen. Cook on high for the last 20–30 minutes of cooking. Seafood is delicious added to garlicky tomato sauce for an easy pasta topper.

Rice-based dishes can be slow cooked, although for best results use easy-cook rice that has been partially cooked first so it is less starchy and so less sticky. If using basmati rice, rinse it in plenty of cold water to remove some of the starch before cooking. When cooking rice, allow a minimum of 250 ml (8 fl oz) water for each 100 g (3½ oz) easy-cook rice, or up to 500 ml (17 fl oz) water

for the same quantity of risotto rice. When making a risotto in the slow cooker, add the hot stock all in one go and adjust with a little extra hot stock at the end if needed. For rice pudding, make with risotto rice, too, as it cooks more quickly than traditional round-grain white pudding rice.

For those who would rather eat less meat or no meat at all, suppers can be based around lentils, pearl barley and canned pulses, which can be added straight to the slow cooker. Dried pulses, beans and split peas need soaking in cold water overnight, then boiling rapidly in water for 10 minutes before draining and cooking in the slow cooker.

slow cooker basics

- Some slow cookers require preheating, others do not; always check the manufacturer's instructions before you begin.
- If cooking food in a basin, individual dishes or a soufflé-style dish, make sure these will fit in your slow cooker pot before you begin making the recipe.
- Foods cooked in a slow cooker must contain liquid; to ensure even cooking press

meat, fish or vegetables below the surface of the liquid.

- Foods will not brown in a slow cooker, so fry foods before they go in or brown the top by transferring the slow cooker pot from its housing to the grill just before serving. Alternatively use a cook's blow torch.
- The smaller the pieces of food, the quicker they will cook.
- Food at the bottom of the slow cooker pot will cook more quickly so put root vegetables into the pot first.
- Don't worry if you get delayed, the food will be fine for an extra hour or so.

do I have to cook things first?

No – meat, fish, vegetables and lentils and grains that don't require soaking first can be put straight into the slow cooker pot but crucially they must then be covered with hot stock or liquid. This saves time and saves you standing over the cooker in your smart work suit before rushing out in the morning. Prepare as much of the recipe as you can the night before – chop or slice onions, cube meat, mix flavourings together and then cover and chill in the refrigerator. However, don't be tempted to part-fry meat the night before and then add cold to the slow cooker the day after.

Pour stock or sauce ingredients into a saucepan and bring to the boil on the hob or microwave in a jug, then pour into the slow cooker and cover and cook. Allow an extra hour or two on to the recipe to make sure that the meat is really tender.

Although not essential, if you have the time, fry the meat first for the best flavour and colour, just as you would if preparing a dish to go into the oven.

how full should the pot be?

A slow cooker is really like a large insulated saucepan and although it must never be used without liquid the amount needed is less than when you are simmering a pan on the hob as there is no danger that a slow cooker will boil dry. As the stew or casserole heats up, the liquid turns to steam, which condenses on the lid and falls back into the pot.

Aim to fill the slow cooker pot between half and three-quarters full. Joints of meat should fill the pot no more than two-thirds full. If using a pudding basin allow 1 cm (½ inch) at the narrowest point in an oval pot or 2 cm (¾ inch) in a round one and then pour hot water into the gap between the basin and the pot so that it comes halfway up the sides. If you are making soup the pot can be a little fuller, but make sure the liquid level is no higher than 2.5 cm (1 inch) from the top.

what setting is best?

Most slow cookers come with two settings – high and low – while others may also have an auto setting or medium or warm setting for greater flexibility. In general, the high setting will take half the time of the low setting. Both settings will reach just below 100°C (212°F), or boiling point, during cooking, but when set to high the temperature is reached more quickly.

An auto setting is not vital but it is helpful if you plan to add meat without frying it first as it will automatically start the slow cooker on high, then reduce to low by means of a thermostat. If your slow cooker doesn't have this then set to high for 30 minutes and then reduce to low manually.

Increasing the temperature from low to high at the end of cooking can also be useful if you want to thicken the casserole with cornflour, add green vegetables, shellfish or dumplings. The warm setting can be used after the cooking time is finished so is ideal for those who want to serve supper in two sittings.

how do you work out timings?

- Most casserole-style dishes made with diced meat, minced meat or chicken leg joints are cooked on low for 8–10 hours.
- Larger items such as joints of meat, pot roasts, turkey drumsticks, lamb shanks and meaty terrines are cooked on high for 5–7 hours.
- Soups are cooked on low for 6–8 hours.
- Egg-style tortillas and frittatas are cooked on low for 2–2½ hours, individual baked eggs on high for 40–50 minutes.
- Baked fish is cooked on low for 1½–2 hours, fish pie on low for 2–3 hours, fish terrine on high for 3–4 hours.
- Rice dishes are cooked on low for 1¾–2 hours.
- Large steamed puds are cooked on high for 4–5 hours, individual ones on high for 2–3 hours.

adjusting the cooking time

If you want to slow down or speed up the timings for diced meat or vegetable casseroles, adjust the heat settings and timings as suggested below:

Low	Medium	High
6–8 hours	4–6 hours	3–4 hours
8–10 hours	6–8 hours	5–6 hours
10–12 hours	8–10 hours	7–8 hours

These timings were taken from the Morphy Richards slow cooker instruction handbook. Do not change timings or settings for fish, whole joints or dairy dishes in recipes.

there seems to be a lot of water around the lid, is this ok?

Yes perfectly – as the slow cooker comes up to temperature the steam condenses and forms a seal around the lid. Every time you lift the lid you break the seal and add an extra 20 minutes to the cooking time. Resist the temptation to lift the lid more than is absolutely necessary. It takes the slow cooker 1 hour to come up to a safe and optimal temperature.

how will I know if the food is ready and cooked through?

This is particularly crucial when cooking meat and fish, but especially when cooking joints. Test as you would if cooking in a conventional

oven by inserting a knife into the centre, or through the thickest part of the leg into the breast if testing a whole chicken. The juices that run out should be clear with no hint of pink and the tip of the knife should feel hot. The knife will also slide into meat easily if tender. For smaller chunks or cubes of meat, take a piece out, cut in half and if done, taste for tenderness. Diced casseroled beef will take considerably longer to cook if it is not fried first.

When testing chicken or duck portions or lamb shanks, the meat will begin to shrink away from the bone when tender; as with the larger joints, press a knife into the thickest part of the joint.

For extra piece of mind a digital meat probe can be a fail-safe way to check as it will tell you exactly the internal temperature of the meat; it can also be used when roasting meat in a traditional oven and some types can be used when making jam, boiling sugar or deep-frying on the hob.

Fish should break easily into even-coloured flakes when pressed in the centre with a knife.

can I use my own recipes?

Of course – to get an idea of timings and amounts that will fit in your slow cooker pot, look up a recipe in the following pages with the same main ingredient and use the amount of liquid suggested in that recipe as a starting point. As a slow cooker uses such gentle heat you will find that you do not need quite the same amount of liquid as you would if making a stove-top stew as there is no danger of a slow cooker drying out.

Nearly all meaty or vegetable stews, casseroles, slow cook curries or chilli can be cooked successfully in the slow cooker; so too can steamed puddings, custards and terrines.

Root vegetables take a surprisingly long time to cook and can take longer to cook than diced beef, especially if the beef has been fried off first. The secret is to cut the vegetables the same size or a little smaller than the meat so that it will all be cooked at the same time, and, if using a mix of different root veggies, to cut them all to a similar size so that they will all be ready at the same time. As the heating elements are in the base and around the sides of the slow cooker, put the vegetables into the slow cooker pot where it will be hottest.

If using a high proportion of fresh tomatoes mixed with stock, reduce the liquid level by one-third or even half, as the tomatoes will give off a lot of juice as they cook down.

If using the slow cooker to steam puddings or to use as a water bath for baked custards or terrines, check that the dish you are going to use will fit into the slow cooker before you begin. You may not be able to fit four standard-sized ramekin dishes into every type of slow cooker, but generally individual dishes that have slightly sloping sides will fit in fine; look out for individual 200 ml (7 fl oz) metal pudding moulds in your local cook shop or try with heatproof tea cups or mugs.

short of time?

Cheat – use a few short cuts such as ready-made cans or jars of sauce – even a can of tomato, chicken or spiced soup can be used as a speedy cook-in-sauce poured over some fried onions, fried chicken pieces or sausages. If you are really short of time then don't fry the meat first – this works best with diced lamb or boneless chicken thighs or ready-made meatballs. Make sure to bring the liquid up to the boil in a saucepan on the hob or in a jug in the microwave before adding. Add everything to the slow cooker pot and cook on high for at least 30 minutes before reducing to low when you go out.

Bought sauces tend to be quite highly seasoned so taste at the end of cooking and adjust with extra salt and pepper just before serving, if needed.

caring for your slow cooker

Because a slow cooker heats food to a lower heat than a conventional oven there are no burnt-on splashes or stubborn marks to get rid of. At the end of cooking, remove the empty earthenware pot from the slow cooker, fill it with warm soapy water and leave to soak, if necessary, then remove any marks with a washing-up brush. Don't stand the pot in water – the unglazed areas are porous and so will soak up water and could then possibly crack when heated in the slow cooker. Some pots are dishwasher safe, but not all, so check with your instruction handbook first.

Wipe out the inside of the slow cooker machine with a damp cloth and a squirt of cream cleanser, making sure that it is unplugged first. Buff up the outside with a dry cloth. Never immerse in water.

safety tips

- Always read the instruction handbook that accompanies your slow cooker before you begin.
- Make sure frozen food is completely defrosted before adding to the slow cooker, with the exception of a small quantity of frozen peas or sweetcorn towards the end of cooking, or frozen fruit.
- Add hot liquid or stock to the slow cooker pot; this is especially important if the meat is not fried first.
- Don't lift the lid off the slow cooker during the first hour of cooking while the slow

cooker heats up to a safe and optimal temperature.

- Lift dishes out of the slow cooker pot using a tea towel or use foil straps (see below).
- The outside of the slow cooker housing gets hot when in use – use oven gloves if removing the pot from the housing as soon as cooking has finished.
- Never reheat already cooked food in a slow cooker.
- Don't leave cooked food to cool down in the turned off slow cooker.

removing a basin from the slow cooker

So that you can easily lift a hot basin out of the slow cooker, tear off two long pieces of foil. Fold each into thirds to make a long, thin strap. Put one on top of the other to make a cross, then sit the pudding basin in the centre. Lift up the straps, then lower the basin into the slow cooker pot carefully. Use the straps to remove the basin at the end of cooking.

soups

vegetable broth with dumplings

Preparation time **35 minutes**
Cooking temperature **low**
Cooking time **8¾–11 hours**
Serves **4**

40 g (1½ oz) **butter**
1 **leek**, sliced; white and
   green parts kept separate
150 g (5 oz) **swede**, diced
150 g (5 oz) **parsnips**, diced
150 g (5 oz) **carrots**, diced
1 **celery stick**, sliced
50 g (2 oz) **pearl barley**
1 litre (1¾ pints) boiling
   vegetable or **chicken stock**
2–3 sprigs of **sage**
1 teaspoon **English mustard**
salt and **pepper**

Dumplings
75 g (3 oz) **self-raising flour**
40 g (1½ oz) **vegetable suet**
2 **streaky bacon rashers**,
   finely diced
about 3 tablespoons **water**

Preheat the slow cooker if necessary; see the manufacturer's instructions. Heat the butter in a large frying pan, add the white leek slices and fry for 2–3 minutes until softened. Stir in the root vegetables and celery and fry for 4–5 minutes.

Add the pearl barley to the slow cooker pot. Then add the fried vegetables, boiling stock and sage. Stir in the mustard and a little salt and pepper. Cover with the lid and cook on low for 8–10 hours or until the vegetables and barley are tender.

Make the dumplings. Put the flour, suet, bacon and a little salt and pepper in a bowl and mix well. Gradually stir in enough water to make a soft but not sticky dough. Knead lightly on a floured surface, then shape into 12 balls.

Stir the reserved green leek slices into the soup, add the dumplings, spacing them slightly apart, then replace the lid and cook, still on low, for 45-60 minutes or until light and fluffy. Ladle into bowls and serve.

For chicken broth with mini herb dumplings, fry
4 small chicken thighs on the bone with the white leek slices. Add the root vegetables and celery, omitting the parsnips. Continue and cook as above for 8–10 hours. Make the dumplings with 2 tablespoons mixed chopped parsley or chives and sage instead of the bacon. Lift the chicken out of the soup, discard the skin and bones and chop the meat into small pieces. Return the meat to the pot with the raw dumplings and green leeks and cook for 45–60 minutes.

mulligatawny soup

Preparation time **15 minutes**
Cooking temperature **low**
Cooking time **6–8 hours**
Serves **4–6**

1 **onion**, chopped
1 **carrot**, diced
1 **dessert apple**, cored and
   coarsely grated
2 **garlic cloves**, finely
   chopped
400 g (13 oz) can **chopped
   tomatoes**
75 g (3 oz) **red lentils**
50 g (2 oz) **sultanas**
3 teaspoons **mild curry paste**
1.2 litres (2 pints) boiling
   vegetable or **chicken stock**
salt and **pepper**

Croutes
50 g (2 oz) **butter**
2 **garlic cloves**, finely
   chopped
3 tablespoons chopped
   coriander
8–12 slices of **French-style
   bread**, depending on size

Preheat the slow cooker if necessary; see the manufacturer's instructions. Put the vegetables, apple, garlic, tomatoes, lentils and sultanas into the slow cooker pot.

Add the curry paste, then stir in the boiling stock and add a little salt and pepper. Cover and cook on low for 6–8 hours or until the lentils are soft and the carrots are tender.

When almost ready to serve, make the croutes. Beat together the butter, garlic and chopped coriander in a bowl. Toast the bread on both sides, then spread with the butter. Ladle the soup into shallow bowls and serve topped with the croutes.

For gingered carrot soup, put 500 g (1 lb) diced carrots and 3.5 cm (1½ inch) peeled and finely chopped fresh root ginger into the slow cooker pot with the onion, lentils and curry paste, omitting the other ingredients. Pour over 1.2 litres (2 pints) boiling vegetable stock and continue as above. Purée with a stick blender, mix in 300 ml (½ pint) milk and cook on high for 15 minutes until piping hot. Ladle into bowls and serve with swirls of natural yogurt.

old english pea & ham soup

Preparation time **15 minutes**
Cooking temperature **high**
Cooking time **5–6 hours**
Serves **4–6**

175 g (6 oz) dried **green split peas**, soaked overnight in cold water
2 **onions**, chopped
2 **celery sticks**, diced
1 **carrot**, diced
1.5 litres (2½ pints) **water**
3 teaspoons **English mustard**
1 **bay leaf**
small **unsmoked boneless bacon joint**, about 500 g (1 lb)
4 tablespoons chopped **parsley**
salt and **pepper**

Preheat the slow cooker if necessary; see the manufacturer's instructions. Drain the peas and add to a large saucepan with the onions, celery, carrot and water. Bring to the boil, skim if needed and boil for 10 minutes.

Pour the mixture into the slow cooker pot, then stir in the mustard, bay leaf and some black pepper. Rinse the bacon joint in several changes of cold water, then add to the pot and press below the surface of the liquid. Cover and cook on high for 5–6 hours or until the peas are soft and the bacon cooked through.

Lift the bacon joint out of the slow cooker pot with a carving fork, drain well, then cut away the rind and fat. Cut the meat into bite-sized pieces. Purée the soup with a stick blender or leave chunky, if preferred. Stir the bacon back into the pot and mix in the parsley. Taste and adjust the seasoning, adding salt, if needed. Ladle the soup into bowls and serve with crusty bread.

For split pea & parsnip soup, soak 175 g (6 oz) yellow split peas as above. Drain and put into a saucepan with 1 chopped onion, 300 g (10 oz) diced parsnips and 1.5 litres (2½ pints) chicken or vegetable stock. Boil for 10 minutes, then transfer to the slow cooker pot. Cover and cook as above. Purée and adjust the seasoning, if needed. Beat 75 g (3 oz) butter with 2 finely chopped garlic cloves, 3 tablespoons chopped coriander, 1 teaspoon roughly crushed cumin seeds and 1 teaspoon roughly crushed coriander seeds. Ladle the soup into bowls and top with spoonfuls of the butter.

chicken & tortelloni soup

Preparation time **15 minutes**
Cooking temperature **high**
Cooking time **5¼–7½ hours**
Serves **4**

1 **chicken carcass**
1 **onion**, quartered
2 **celery sticks**, sliced
2 **carrots**, thinly sliced
2 sprigs of **thyme** or **basil**
1.25 litres (2¼ pints) boiling
  water
½ teaspoon **black**
  peppercorns, roughly
  crushed
salt
100 g (3½ oz) **spinach**,
  washed, drained and
  roughly torn
3 **tomatoes**, diced
250 g (8 oz) fresh **spinach**
  tortelloni
freshly grated **Parmesan**
  cheese, to serve

Preheat the slow cooker if necessary; see the
manufacturer's instructions. Put the chicken carcass
into the slow cooker pot, breaking it in half if needed.
Add the vegetables, herbs and boiling water, then add
the peppercorns and salt.

Cover with the lid and cook on high for 5–7 hours. Lift
the carcass out of the slow cooker pot and remove any
meat; cut this into small pieces and reserve. Strain the
stock, discarding the bones, vegetables and herbs, then
pour the hot stock back into the slow cooker pot.

Add the shredded chicken, spinach, tomatoes and
tortelloni. Replace the lid and cook for 20–30 minutes,
still on high, until piping hot. Ladle the soup into bowls
and serve sprinkled with a little grated Parmesan.

For pesto & lemon soup, cook the chicken carcass
as above, then stir 2 teaspoons pesto sauce and the
grated rind and juice of 1 lemon into the strained
stock. Mix in 125 g (4 oz) finely chopped broccoli,
125 g (4 oz) frozen peas and 125 g (4 oz) roughly
chopped spinach with the shredded chicken, omitting
the tomatoes and tortelloni. Cook as above and serve
topped with extra pesto and grated Parmesan.

haddock & bacon chowder

Preparation time **15 minutes**
Cooking temperature **high**
Cooking time **2½–3½ hours**
Serves **4**

25 g (1 oz) **butter**
1 **onion**, finely chopped
300 g (10 oz) **potatoes**, cut
   into small dice
4 **smoked streaky bacon
   rashers**, diced
750 ml (1¼ pints) boiling **fish
   stock**
125 g (4 oz) frozen
   sweetcorn, thawed
1 **bay leaf**
500 g (1 lb) **smoked
   haddock**, skinned
150 ml (¼ pint) **double cream**
salt and **pepper**
chopped **parsley**, to garnish

Preheat the slow cooker if necessary; see the
manufacturer's instructions. Heat the butter in a large
frying pan, add the onion, potatoes and bacon and fry
gently, stirring, until just beginning to colour.

Transfer the potato mixture to the slow cooker pot.
Pour over the boiling stock, then add the sweetcorn,
bay leaf and a little salt and pepper. Cover with the lid
and cook on high for 2–3 hours or until the potatoes
are tender.

Add the fish and press it just below the surface of the
stock, cutting the pieces in half, if needed. Replace
the lid and cook, still on high, for 30 minutes or until
the fish flakes easily when pressed in the centre with
a knife.

Lift the fish on to a plate with a fish slice and break it
into flakes with a knife and fork, checking for and
removing any bones. Stir the cream into the soup, then
return the fish. Ladle the soup into bowls and sprinkle
with parsley.

For salmon & crab chowder, fry the onion and
potatoes, omitting the bacon, and continue and cook
for 2–3 hours as above. Replace the smoked haddock
with a 43 g (1¾ oz) can dressed brown crab meat,
stirred into the potato mixture, and 500 g (1 lb)
salmon fillet, cut into 4 strips and pressed below the
surface of the stock. Cook for 30–40 minutes until
salmon is cooked, then continue as above.

thai coconut & pumpkin soup

Preparation time **20 minutes**
Cooking temperature **low**
Cooking time **7–8 hours**
Serves **4–6**

1 tablespoon **sunflower oil**
1 **onion**, chopped
4 teaspoons **Thai red curry paste**
1 teaspoon **galangal paste**
2 **garlic cloves**, finely chopped
1 **butternut squash**, about 1 kg (2 lb), peeled, deseeded and cut into 2 cm (¾ inch) chunks
250 ml (8 fl oz) carton **coconut cream**
750 ml (1¼ pint) **vegetable stock**
1 tablespoon **soy sauce**
small bunch of **coriander**
salt and **pepper**

Preheat the slow cooker if necessary; see the manufacturer's instructions. Heat the oil in a large frying pan, add the onion and fry until softened. Stir in the curry paste, galangal and garlic and cook for 1 minute, then mix in the squash.

Pour in the coconut cream and stock, then add the soy sauce and bring to the boil, stirring. Pour into the slow cooker pot, cover with the lid and cook on low for 7–8 hours or until the squash is tender. (You may find that the coconut cream separates slightly but this will disappear after puréeing.)

Purée the soup while still in the slow cooker pot with a stick blender. Alternatively, transfer to a liquidizer and purée, in batches if necessary, until smooth, then return it to the slow cooker pot and reheat on high for 15 minutes.

Reserve a few sprigs of coriander for garnish, chop the rest and stir into the soup. Ladle the soup into bowls and garnish with the reserved coriander sprigs.

For pumpkin & orange soup, fry the onion in 25 g (1 oz) butter, then add the diced butternut squash with the grated rind and juice of 2 small oranges, 900 ml (1½ pints) vegetable stock and 3 whole star anise. Bring to the boil, stirring, add a little salt and pepper and continue as above. Remove the star anise before puréeing and serve with swirls of double cream.

tomato & red pepper soup

Preparation time **15 minutes**
Cooking temperature **high**
Cooking time **2½–3 hours**
Serves **4–6**

2 tablespoons **olive oil**
1 **onion**, chopped
1 **red pepper**, cored,
   deseeded and diced
750 g (1½ lb) **tomatoes**,
   roughly chopped
1 **garlic clove**, finely chopped
600 ml (1 pint) **vegetable
   stock**
1 tablespoon **tomato purée**
2 teaspoons **caster sugar**
1 tablespoon **balsamic
   vinegar**, plus extra to garnish
salt and **pepper**

Preheat the slow cooker if necessary; see the manufacturer's instructions. Heat the oil in a large frying pan, add the onion and fry until softened. Stir in the red pepper, tomatoes and garlic and fry for 1–2 minutes.

Pour in the stock and add the tomato purée, sugar, vinegar and a little salt and pepper and bring to the boil, stirring. Pour into the slow cooker pot, cover with the lid and cook on high for 2½–3 hours or until the vegetables are tender.

Purée the soup while still in the slow cooker pot with a stick blender. Alternatively, transfer to a liquidizer and purée, in batches if necessary, until smooth, then return to the slow cooker pot and reheat on high for 15 minutes.

Taste and adjust the seasoning, if needed, then ladle the soup into bowls and garnish with a drizzle of extra vinegar or stir in spoonfuls of spring onion pesto (see below).

For spring onion & basil pesto to garnish the soup, roughly chop 4 spring onions, then finely chop with a stick blender in a jug, or in a liquidizer, with 4 sprigs of basil, 25 g (1 oz) freshly grated Parmesan, 4 tablespoons olive oil and a little pepper until a coarse paste. Spoon over the top of the soup just before serving.

lamb & barley broth

Preparation time **15 minutes**
Cooking temperature **low**
Cooking time **8–10 hours**
Serves **4–6**

25 g (1 oz) **butter**
1 tablespoon **sunflower oil**
1 **lamb rump chop** or 125 g
    (4 oz) **lamb fillet**, diced
1 **onion**, chopped
1 small **leek**, chopped
500 g (1 lb) mixed **parsnip,
    swede, turnip** and **carrot**,
    cut into small dice
50 g (2 oz) **pearl barley**
1.2 litres (2 pints) **lamb** or
    chicken stock
¼ teaspoon **ground allspice**
2–3 sprigs of **rosemary**
salt and **pepper**
chopped **parsley** or **chives**, to
    garnish (optional)

Preheat the slow cooker if necessary; see the manufacturer's instructions. Heat the butter and oil in a large frying pan, add the lamb, onion and leek and fry, stirring, until the lamb is lightly browned.

Stir in the root vegetables and barley, then add the stock, allspice, rosemary and plenty of salt and pepper and bring to the boil, stirring. Pour into the slow cooker pot, cover with the lid and cook on low for 8–10 hours or until the barley is tender.

Stir well, taste and adjust the seasoning, if needed, then ladle the soup into bowls. Garnish with chopped herbs, if liked, and serve with warm bread.

For Hungarian chorba, fry the lamb and vegetables as above, omitting the pearl barley. Stir in 1 teaspoon smoked paprika, then add 50 g (2 oz) long-grain rice and a few sprigs of dill. Stir in 1.2 litres (2 pints) lamb stock, 2 tablespoons red wine vinegar and 1 tablespoon light muscovado sugar. Add salt and pepper, bring to the boil and continue as above. Garnish with extra chopped dill and serve with rye bread.

carrot & cumin soup

Preparation time **20 minutes**
Cooking temperature **low**
Cooking time **7–8 hours**
Serves **4–6**

1 tablespoon **sunflower oil**
1 large **onion**, chopped
625 g (1¼ lb) **carrots**, thinly
    sliced
1½ teaspoons **cumin seeds**,
    roughly crushed
1 teaspoon **turmeric**
50 g (2 oz) **long-grain rice**
1.2 litres (2 pints) **vegetable
    stock**
salt and **pepper**

To serve
150 g (5 oz) **natural yogurt**
mango chutney
a few **poppadums**

Preheat the slow cooker if necessary; see the manufacturer's instructions. Heat the oil in a large frying pan, add the onion and fry over a medium heat, stirring, until softened. Stir in the carrots, cumin seeds and turmeric and fry for 2–3 minutes to release the cumin flavour and colour the onions.

Stir in the rice, then add the stock and a little salt and pepper and bring to the boil. Pour into the slow cooker pot, cover with the lid and cook on low for 7–8 hours or until the carrots are tender.

Purée the soup while still in the slow cooker pot with a stick blender. Alternatively, transfer to a liquidizer and purée, in batches if necessary, until smooth, then return to the slow cooker pot and reheat on high for 15 minutes.

Taste and adjust the seasoning, if needed, then ladle the soup into bowls. Top with spoonfuls of yogurt and a little mango chutney and serve with poppadums.

For spiced parsnip soup, fry the onion as above, replacing the carrots with 625 g (1¼ lb) halved and thinly sliced parsnips and adding 1 teaspoon turmeric, 1 teaspoon ground cumin, 1 teaspoon ground coriander and 3.5 cm (1½ inch) peeled and finely chopped fresh root ginger. Continue as above.

minestrone soup

Preparation time **15 minutes**
Cooking temperature **low** and
high
Cooking time **6¼–8½ hours**
Serves **4**

1 tablespoon **olive oil**
1 **onion**, chopped
1 **carrot**, diced
2 **smoked streaky bacon**
rashers, diced
2 **garlic cloves**, finely
chopped
4 **tomatoes**, skinned and
chopped
2 **celery sticks**, diced
2 small **courgettes**, diced
3 teaspoons **pesto**, plus extra
to serve
1.2 litres (2 pints) **chicken** or
vegetable stock
75 g (3 oz) **purple sprouting**
broccoli, stems and florets
cut into small pieces
40 g (1½ oz) tiny **soup pasta**
salt and **pepper**
freshly grated **Parmesan**
cheese, to serve

Preheat the slow cooker if necessary; see the manufacturer's instructions. Heat the oil in a large frying pan, add the onion, carrot and bacon and fry, stirring, until lightly browned.

Add the garlic, then stir in the tomatoes, celery and courgettes and cook for 1–2 minutes. Stir in the pesto and stock, then add a little salt and pepper and bring to the boil, stirring.

Pour into the slow cooker pot, cover with the lid and cook on low for 6–8 hours or until the vegetables are tender. Add the broccoli and pasta, replace the lid and cook on high for 15–30 minutes or until the pasta is tender.

Stir well, taste and adjust the seasoning, if needed, then ladle the soup into bowls. Top with extra spoonfuls of pesto, to taste, and sprinkle with grated Parmesan. Serve with crusty bread.

For curried vegetable & chicken soup, omit the bacon and add the diced meat from 2 chicken thighs when frying the onion and carrot. Add the garlic, tomatoes, celery and courgette, then add 3 teaspoons mild curry paste instead of the pesto and 40 g (1½ oz) basmati rice. Add 1.2 litres (2 pints) chicken stock and continue as above, omitting the pasta. Garnish with chopped coriander and serve with warmed naan breads.

leek, potato & stilton soup

Preparation time **25 minutes**
Cooking temperature **low**
Cooking time **5½–6½ hours**
Serves 4–6

25 g (1 oz) **butter**
1 tablespoon **sunflower oil**
500 g (1 lb) **leeks**, thinly
  sliced; white and green parts
  kept separate
1 **smoked back bacon
  rasher**, diced, plus
  4 grilled **rashers**, chopped,
  to garnish
375 g (12 oz) **potatoes**, diced
900 ml (1½ pints) **chicken** or
  vegetable stock
300 ml (½ pint) **milk**
150 ml (¼ pint) **double cream**
150 g (5 oz) **mature Stilton**
  (rind removed), diced
salt and **pepper**

Preheat the slow cooker if necessary; see the manufacturer's instructions. Heat the butter and oil in a large frying pan, then add the white leek slices, the diced bacon and potatoes and fry over a medium heat, stirring, until just beginning to turn golden.

Pour in the stock, add a little salt and pepper and bring to the boil, stirring. Transfer to the slow cooker pot, cover with the lid and cook on low for 5–6 hours. Stir the reserved green leek slices and milk into the slow cooker pot. Replace the lid and cook, still on low, for 30 minutes or until the leeks are tender. Roughly purée the soup in the pot with a stick blender or use a masher, if preferred.

Mix in the cream and two-thirds of the cheese and continue stirring until the cheese has melted. Taste and adjust the seasoning, if needed, then ladle the soup into bowls and sprinkle with the remaining cheese and chopped grilled bacon.

For cock-a-leekie soup, heat the butter and oil as above, then add 2 chicken thighs on the bone and fry until golden, remove them from pan and put into the slow cooker pot. Fry the leeks, bacon and potatoes as above, then mix in 1.2 litres (2 pints) chicken stock, 50 g (2 oz) stoned chopped prunes and a sprig of thyme. Season, bring to the boil, then transfer to the pot. Cover and cook on low for 8–10 hours. Take the chicken off the bone, discarding the skin, then dice the meat and return it to the pot with the green leek slices. Cook for 30 minutes, then ladle into bowls. Omit the milk, cream, Stilton and bacon garnish.

crab gumbo

Preparation time **15 minutes**
Cooking temperature **high**
Cooking time **3¼ hours–4½
hours**
Serves **4**

1 tablespoon **sunflower oil**
1 **onion**, finely chopped
1 **garlic clove**, chopped
2 **celery sticks**, sliced
1 **carrot**, cut into small dice
400 g (13 oz) can **chopped
tomatoes**
600 ml (1 pint) **fish stock**
50 g (2 oz) easy-cook **long-
grain rice**
1 **bay leaf**
2 sprigs of **thyme**
¼ teaspoon **crushed dried
red chillies**
75 g (3 oz) **okra**, sliced
43 g (1¾ oz) can **dressed
brown crab meat**
salt and **pepper**
170 g (5¾ oz) can **white crab
meat**, to serve (optional)

Preheat the slow cooker if necessary; see the
manufacturer's instructions. Heat the oil in a large frying
pan, add the onion and fry for 5 minutes or until
softened.

Stir in the garlic, celery and carrot, then mix in the
tomatoes, stock, rice, herbs and chillies. Add a little salt
and pepper and bring to the boil. Pour into the slow
cooker pot, cover with the lid and cook on high for
3–4 hours or until the vegetables and rice are tender.

Stir the soup, then add the okra and dressed brown
crab meat. Replace the lid and cook, still on high, for
20–30 minutes. Ladle the soup into bowls, top with the
flaked white crab meat, if liked, and serve with warm
crusty bread.

For mixed vegetable gumbo, make up the soup
as above, omitting the cans of brown and white crab
meat. Garnish with croutons made by frying 2 slices
of bread, cut into cubes, in 25 g (1 oz) butter,
3 tablespoons olive oil and ¼ teaspoon crushed dried
red chillies until golden.

caramelized onion soup

Preparation time **25 minutes**
Cooking temperature **low**
Cooking time **4–5 hours**
Serves **4**

25 g (1 oz) **butter**
2 tablespoons **olive oil**
500 g (1 lb) **onions**, thinly
    sliced
1 tablespoon **caster sugar**
2 tablespoons **plain flour**
250 ml (8 fl oz) **brown ale**
750 ml (1¼ pints) **beef stock**
2 **bay leaves**
1 tablespoon **Worcestershire
    sauce**
salt and **pepper**

Cheesy croutes
8 slices of **French bread**
75 g (3 oz) **mature Cheddar
    cheese**, grated
2 teaspoons **Worcestershire
    sauce**

Preheat the slow cooker if necessary; see the manufacturer's instructions. Heat the butter and oil in a large frying pan, add the onions and fry over a medium heat, stirring occasionally, for 15 minutes or until softened and just beginning to turn golden. Stir in the sugar and fry for 10 minutes, stirring frequently as the onions begin to caramelize and turn a deep golden brown.

Stir in the flour, then add the ale, stock, bay leaves and Worcestershire sauce. Add a little salt and pepper and bring to the boil, stirring. Pour into the slow cooker pot, cover with the lid and cook on low for 4–5 hours or until the onions are very soft.

When almost ready to serve, toast the French bread slices on both sides, sprinkle with the cheese and drizzle with the Worcestershire sauce. Grill until the cheese is bubbling. Ladle the soup into shallow bowls and float the croutes on top.

For French onion soup, fry the onions as above and stir in the flour. Replace the ale with 250 ml (8 fl oz) red wine and add with the stock, bay leaves and salt and pepper, omitting the Worcestershire sauce. Continue as above. For the croutes, toast the French bread, then rub one side of each piece with a cut garlic clove and sprinkle with 75 g (3 oz) grated Gruyère cheese and grill. Serve as above.

tomato, lentil & aubergine soup

Preparation time **20 minutes**
Cooking temperature **low**
Cooking time **6–8 hours**
Serves **4**

4 tablespoons **olive oil**, plus
   extra to garnish (optional)
1 **aubergine**, sliced
1 **onion**, chopped
2 **garlic cloves**, finely
   chopped
½ teaspoon **smoked paprika**
1 teaspoon **ground cumin**
125 g (4 oz) **red lentils**
400 g (13 oz) can **chopped
   tomatoes**
750 ml (1 ¼ pints) boiling
   vegetable stock
salt and **pepper**
chopped **coriander**, to garnish

Preheat the slow cooker if necessary; see the
manufacturer's instructions. Heat 1 tablespoon of the
oil in a large frying pan, add one-third of the aubergines
and fry on both sides until softened and golden. Scoop
out of the pan with a slotted spoon and transfer to a
plate. Repeat with the rest of the aubergines using
2 more tablespoons of oil.

Add the remaining oil to the pan and fry the onion for
5 minutes or until softened. Stir in the garlic, paprika
and cumin and cook for 1 minute, then mix in the lentils
and tomatoes. Add a little salt and pepper and bring to
the boil. Pour the mixture into the slow cooker pot and
stir in the boiling stock.

Cover with the lid and cook on low for 6–8 hours.
Serve the soup as it is or purée it with a stick blender,
if preferred. Ladle the soup into bowls, drizzle with a
little extra olive oil and sprinkle with coriander. Serve
with toasted ciabatta bread.

For tomato, lentil & chorizo soup, omit the
aubergine and fry the onion in 1 tablespoon olive oil.
Add the garlic, paprika and ground cumin, then stir in
1 cored, deseeded and diced red pepper and 50 g
(2 oz) diced chorizo and fry for 2 minutes. Continue
as above.

thai broth with fish dumplings

Preparation time **30 minutes**
Cooking temperature **low** and
high
Cooking time **2¼–3¼ hours**
Serves **4**

900 ml (1½ pints) boiling **fish
stock**
2 teaspoons **Thai fish sauce**
(nam pla)
1 tablespoon **Thai red curry
paste**
1 tablespoon **soy sauce**
1 **carrot**, thinly sliced
2 **garlic cloves**, finely
chopped
1 bunch of **asparagus**,
trimmed and stems
cut into 4
2 **pak choi**, thickly sliced

Dumplings
1 bunch of **spring onions**,
sliced
15 g (½ oz) **coriander leaves**
3.5 cm (1½ inches) **fresh root
ginger**, peeled and sliced
400 g (13 oz) **cod**, skinned
1 tablespoon **cornflour**
1 **egg white**

Preheat the slow cooker if necessary; see the
manufacturer's instructions. Make the dumplings. Put
half of the spring onions into a food processor with the
coriander and ginger and chop finely. Add the cod,
cornflour and egg white and process until the fish is
finely chopped. With wetted hands, shape the mixture
into 12 balls.

Pour the boiling fish stock into the slow cooker pot,
add the fish sauce, curry paste and soy sauce. Add the
rest of the spring onions, the carrot and garlic and drop
in the dumplings. Cover with the lid and cook on low for
2–3 hours.

When almost ready to serve, add the asparagus and
pak choi to the broth. Replace the lid and cook on high
for 15 minutes or until just tender. Ladle into bowls
and serve.

For Thai broth with noodles & prawns, prepare and
cook the broth as above, omitting the dumplings, for
2–3 hours. Add the asparagus, pak choi and 200 g
(7 oz) frozen large prawns, thoroughly thawed, and
cook for 15 minutes on high. Meanwhile, soak 75 g
(3 oz) rice noodles in boiling water according to the
pack instructions. Drain and add to the bottom of
4 soup bowls. Ladle the broth on top and sprinkle
with a little chopped coriander.

cheesy cauliflower soup

Preparation time **20 minutes**
Cooking temperature **low and high**
Cooking time **4¼–5¼ hours**
Serves **4**

25 g (1 oz) **butter**
1 tablespoon **olive oil**
1 **onion**, chopped
1 small **baking potato**, about 150 g (5 oz), cut into small dice
1 **cauliflower**, trimmed and cut into pieces, about 500 g (1 lb) prepared weight
600 ml (1 pint) **vegetable stock**
1 teaspoon **English mustard**
3 teaspoons **Worcestershire sauce**
50 g (2 oz) **Parmesan** or **mature Cheddar cheese**, grated
200 ml (7 fl oz) **milk**
grated **nutmeg**
salt and **pepper**

To serve
150 ml (¼ pint) **double cream**
croutons

Preheat the slow cooker if necessary; see the manufacturer's instructions. Heat the butter and oil in a large frying pan, add the onion and potato and fry for 5 minutes or until softened but not coloured.

Stir in the cauliflower, stock, mustard, Worcestershire sauce, cheese and a little salt and pepper and bring to the boil. Pour into the slow cooker pot, cover with the lid and cook on low for 4–5 hours or until the vegetables are tender.

Purée the soup while still in the slow cooker pot with a stick blender. Alternatively, transfer to a liquidizer and purée, in batches if necessary, until smooth, then return to the slow cooker pot.

Stir in the milk, replace the lid and cook on high for 15 minutes until reheated. Stir and add nutmeg to taste. Ladle the soup into bowls, swirl cream over the top and sprinkle with a little extra grated nutmeg and some croutons.

For cheesy pumpkin soup, omit the cauliflower and add 500 g (1 lb) peeled and deseeded pumpkin or butternut squash. Dice the flesh and add to the fried onion and potato mixture. Continue as above.

light bites & everyday suppers

garlicky pork & sage pâté

Preparation time **30 minutes**, plus overnight chilling
Cooking temperature **high**
Cooking time **5–6 hours**
Serves **6–8**

1 tablespoon **olive oil**, plus extra for greasing
1 bunch of **sage**
1 small **onion**, chopped
400 g (13 oz) or 6 **Toulouse sausages**, skins slit and removed
75 g (3 oz) **smoked streaky bacon**, diced
200 g (7 oz) boneless **belly pork** rashers, finely diced
150 g (5 oz) **chicken livers**, rinsed with cold water and drained
1 **egg**, beaten
2 tablespoons **sherry vinegar**
salt and **pepper**

Preheat the slow cooker if necessary; see the manufacturer's instructions. Oil a 900 ml (1½ pint) rectangular heatproof dish and line the base and two long sides with nonstick baking paper, checking first that it will fit in the slow cooker pot. Cover the base with sage leaves, reserving the remainder.

Heat the oil in a frying pan, add the onion and fry until softened. Transfer to a bowl and add the sausages, bacon and diced pork. Chop the drained chicken livers, discarding the white cores. Add to the bowl with the egg, vinegar and plenty of salt and pepper. Mix together, then spoon half the mixture into the dish and press down firmly.

Arrange more sage leaves over the pâté, then cover with the remaining mixture. Press down firmly and arrange any remaining sage leaves on the top. Cover loosely with foil and stand the dish in the slow cooker pot. Pour boiling water into the pot to come halfway up the sides of the dish. Cover with the lid or foil, and cook on high for 5–6 hours or until the meat juices run clear when the centre of the pâté is pierced with a knife.

Lift the dish out of the slow cooker pot using a tea towel, pour off the excess fat, stand the dish on a plate, then cover the top with a second plate and weigh down with measuring weights. Leave to cool, then transfer to the refrigerator overnight.

To serve, remove the weights, plate and foil. Loosen the edges of the pâté with a knife, then turn out on to a chopping board and peel off the lining paper. Cut into slices and serve with toasted bread and salad.

red pepper & chorizo tortilla

Preparation time **20 minutes**
Cooking temperature **high**
Cooking time **2–2½ hours**
Serves **4**

1 tablespoon **olive oil**, plus
    extra for greasing
1 small **onion**, chopped
75 g (3 oz) **chorizo**, diced
6 **eggs**
150 ml (¼ pint) **milk**
100 g (3½ oz) roasted **red**
    pepper (from a jar), drained
    and sliced
250 g (8 oz) cooked
    potatoes, sliced
salt and **pepper**

Preheat the slow cooker if necessary; see the
manufacturer's instructions. Lightly oil a 1.2 litre
(2 pint) soufflé dish and base-line with a circle of
nonstick baking paper, checking first that the dish will
fit in the slow cooker pot.

Heat the oil in a frying pan, add the onion and chorizo
and fry for 4–5 minutes until the onion is softened.
Beat the eggs, milk and a little salt and pepper in a
bowl, then add the onion and chorizo, the red pepper
and sliced potatoes and mix together.

Tip the mixture into the oiled dish, cover the top with
foil and stand the dish in the slow cooker pot. Pour
boiling water into the pot to come halfway up the
sides of the dish. Cover with the lid and cook on high
for 2–2½ hours or until the egg mixture has set in
the centre.

Lift the dish out of the slow cooker pot using a tea
towel and remove the foil. Loosen the edge of the
tortilla with a knife, turn it out on to a plate and peel off
the lining paper. Cut into slices and serve hot or cold
with salad.

For cheesy bacon & rosemary tortilla, replace the
chorizo with 75 g (3 oz) diced smoked streaky bacon
and fry with the onion as above. Beat the eggs and
milk in a bowl with the chopped leaves from 2 small
rosemary sprigs and 4 tablespoons freshly grated
Parmesan or Cheddar cheese and salt and pepper.
Replace the red pepper with 75 g (3 oz) sliced button
mushrooms and continue as above.

baked eggs on toast

Preparation time **15 minutes**
Cooking temperature **high**
Cooking time **40–50 minutes**
Serves **4**

25 g (1 oz) **butter**
4 wafer thin slices of **honey
    roast ham**, about 65 g
    (2½ oz) in total
4 teaspoons **spicy tomato
    chutney**
4 **eggs**
2 **cherry tomatoes**, halved
1 **spring onion**, finely sliced
salt and **pepper**
4 slices of **buttered toast**,
    to serve

Preheat the slow cooker if necessary; see the
manufacturer's instructions. Grease 4 heatproof dishes,
each 150 ml (5 fl oz), with a little of the butter,
checking first they will fit in the slow cooker pot, then
press a slice of ham into each to line the base and
sides, leaving a small overhang of ham above the dish.

Add 1 teaspoon of chutney to the base of each dish,
then break an egg on top. Add a cherry tomato half to
each, sprinkle with the spring onion and a little salt and
pepper, then dot with the remaining butter.

Cover each one with a square of foil and put the dishes
into the slow cooker pot. Pour boiling water into the pot
to come halfway up the sides of the dishes. Cover with
the lid and cook on high for 40–50 minutes or until the
egg whites are set and the yolks still slightly soft.

Lift the dishes out of the slow cooker pot using a tea
towel and remove the foil. Loosen between the ham and
the edge of the dishes with a knife and turn out. Quickly
turn the baked eggs the right way up and arrange each
one on a plate with hot buttered toast fingers.

For eggs Benedict, butter 4 dishes as above, then
break an egg into each one, sprinkle with salt and
pepper, the sliced spring onion and remaining butter.
Cover with foil and cook as above. To serve, grill
8 back bacon rashers until golden. Toast 4 halved
English breakfast muffins, spread with butter, divide
the bacon between the lower halves and arrange on
serving plates. Top with the baked eggs and remaining
muffin halves and serve drizzled with 150 ml (¼ pint)
warmed ready-made hollandaise sauce.

fish terrine

Preparation time **30 minutes**,
   plus cooling
Cooking temperature **high**
Cooking time **3–4 hours**
Serves **6–8**

oil, for greasing
375 g (12 oz) boneless
   haddock or **cod loin**, cubed
2 **egg whites**
grated rind of ½ **lemon**
juice of 1 **lemon**
250 ml (8 fl oz) **double cream**
125 g (4 oz) sliced **smoked
   salmon** or **trout**
150 g (5 oz) **salmon** or **trout
   fillet**, thinly sliced
salt and **pepper**

Preheat the slow cooker if necessary; see the manufacturer's instructions. Lightly oil a 1 litre (1¾ pint) soufflé dish and base-line with a circle of nonstick baking paper, checking first that the dish will fit in the slow cooker pot. Blend the haddock or cod loin, egg whites, lemon rind, half the lemon juice and salt and pepper in a food processor until roughly chopped, then gradually add the cream and blend until just beginning to thicken.

Arrange half the smoked fish slices over the base of the dish. Spoon in half the fish mousse and spread it level. Mix the fish fillet with a little remaining lemon juice and some pepper, then arrange on top. Top with the remaining fish mousse, then the smoked fish slices.

Cover the top with foil and lower into the slow cooker pot. Pour boiling water into the pot to come halfway up the sides of the dish. Cover with the lid and cook on high for 3–4 hours or until the fish is cooked through and the terrine is set.

Lift the dish out of the slow cooker pot using a tea towel and leave to cool for 2 hours. Loosen the edge, turn out on to a plate and peel off the lining paper. Cut into thick slices and serve with salad and toast.

For smoked haddock & chive terrine make up the white fish mousse as above and flavour with 4 tablespoons chopped chives, 2 tablespoons chopped capers and the grated rind and juice of half a lemon. Omit the smoked fish and arrange 1 sliced tomato over the base of the dish. Cover with half the fish mousse, 150 g (5 oz) thinly sliced smoked cod fillet, then the remaining fish mousse. Continue as above.

warm lentil & feta salad

Preparation time **20 minutes**
Cooking temperature **high**
Cooking time **3–4 hours**
Serves **4**

150 g (5 oz) **puy lentils**
1 **onion**, chopped
1 **red pepper**, cored,
 deseeded and sliced
250 g (8 oz) **cherry tomatoes**
600 ml (1 pint) boiling **water**
2 tablespoons **tomato purée**
2 sprigs of **thyme**
4 tablespoons **olive oil**
2 tablespoons **balsamic**
 vinegar
100 g (3½ oz) bag
 watercress, spinach and
 rocket salad
150 g (5 oz) **feta cheese**,
 crumbled
small bunch of **mint**, leaves
 stripped from the stems
salt and **pepper**

Preheat the slow cooker if necessary; see the manufacturer's instructions. Put the lentils into a sieve, rinse well with cold water, drain and add to the slow cooker pot along with the onion, red pepper and tomatoes.

Mix the boiling stock with the tomato purée, thyme and a generous amount of salt and pepper. Pour over the lentils, cover with the lid and cook on high for 3–4 hours or until the lentils are tender.

When almost ready to serve, fork the oil and balsamic vinegar together in a bowl, add the salad leaves and toss gently. Spoon the hot lentils into shallow bowls, draining off any excess cooking liquid. Pile the salad on top and sprinkle with the feta, mint leaves and a little extra pepper. Serve immediately with warm pitta breads. Alternatively, lift the pot out of the housing using oven gloves, leave the lentils to go cold, then make the dressing and toss together with the leaves, feta and mint.

For lentil salad with sardines & peas, cook the lentils as above, adding 100 g (3½ oz) frozen peas for the last 15 minutes of cooking time. Drain 2 x 120 g (3¾ oz) cans sardines in tomato sauce, reserving the sauce. Flake the fish into chunky pieces, discarding the bones. Stir the sauce into the lentils. Shred 2 little gem lettuces and mix with ½ finely chopped red onion, then toss with the juice of 1 lemon, a small bunch of roughly chopped mint and salt and pepper. Spoon the hot lentils into shallow bowls, top with the sardines and the lettuce salad. Serve immediately.

duck, pork & apple rillettes

Preparation time **30 minutes**, plus cooling and overnight chilling
Cooking temperature **high**
Cooking time **5–6 hours**
Serves **4**

2 **duck legs**
500 g (1 lb) rindless **belly pork rashers**, halved
1 **onion**, cut into wedges
1 sharp **dessert apple**, such as Granny Smith, peeled, cored and thickly sliced
2–3 sprigs of **thyme**
250 ml (8 fl oz) **chicken stock**
150 ml (¼ pint) **dry cider**
salt and **pepper**

Preheat the slow cooker if necessary; see the manufacturer's instructions. Put the duck and belly pork into the base of the slow cooker pot. Tuck the onion and apple between the pieces of meat and add the thyme.

Pour the stock and cider into a saucepan and add plenty of salt and pepper. Bring to the boil, then pour into the slow cooker pot. Cover with the lid and cook on high for 5–6 hours or until the duck and pork are cooked through and tender.

Lift the meat out of the slow cooker pot with a slotted spoon and transfer to a large plate, then leave to cool for 30 minutes. Peel away the duck skin and remove the bones. Shred the meat into small pieces and discard the thyme sprigs. Scoop out the apple and onion with a slotted spoon, finely chop and mix with the meat, then taste and adjust the seasoning, if needed.

Pack the chopped meat mix into 4 individual dishes or small 'le parfait' jars and press down firmly. Spoon over the juices from the slow cooker pot to cover and seal the meat. Leave to cool, then transfer to the refrigerator and chill well.

When the fat has solidified on the top, cover each dish with a lid or clingfilm and store in the refrigerator for up to 1 week. Serve the rillettes with warm crusty bread, a few radishes and pickled shallots, if liked.

For chicken, pork & prune rillettes, omit the duck and put 2 chicken leg joints into the slow cooker pot with the belly pork rashers, onion and thyme, replacing the apple with 75 g (3 oz) ready-to-eat stoned prunes. Continue as above.

turkey & cranberry meatloaf

Preparation time **30 minutes**,
plus overnight chilling
Cooking temperature **high**
Cooking time **5–6 hours**
Serves **4–6**

1 tablespoon **sunflower oil**,
plus extra for greasing
200 g (7 oz) **smoked streaky
bacon rashers**
115 g (3¾ oz) pack dried
**orange and cranberry
stuffing mix**
25 g (1 oz) dried **cranberries**
1 **onion**, finely chopped
500 g (1 lb) skinless **turkey
breast steaks**
1 **egg**, beaten
salt and **pepper**

Preheat the slow cooker if necessary; see the manufacturer's instructions. Lightly oil a soufflé dish, 14 cm (5½ inches) in diameter and 9 cm (3½ inches) high, and base-line with nonstick baking paper, checking first that the dish will fit in the slow cooker pot. Stretch each bacon rasher with the flat of a large cook's knife, until half as long again, and use about three-quarters of the rashers to line the base and sides of the dish, trimming to fit.

Put the stuffing mix in a bowl, add the cranberries and mix with boiling water according to the pack instructions. Heat the oil in a frying pan, add the onion and fry for 5 minutes, stirring, until softened. Set aside. Finely chop the turkey slices in a food processor or pass through a coarse mincer.

Mix the stuffing with the fried onion, chopped turkey and egg. Season well and spoon into the bacon-lined dish. Press flat and cover with the remaining bacon rashers. Cover the top of the dish with foil and lower into the slow cooker pot. Pour boiling water into the pot to come halfway up the sides of the dish. Cover with the lid and cook on high for 5–6 hours or until the juices run clear when the centre of the meatloaf is pierced with a knife.

Lift the dish out of the slow cooker pot using a tea towel and leave to cool. Transfer to the refrigerator to chill overnight until firm. Loosen the edge of the meatloaf with a knife, turn out on to a plate and peel off the lining paper. Cut into thick slices and serve with salad and spoonfuls of cranberry sauce or Beetroot Chutney (see pages 214–215), if liked.

courgette & broad bean frittata

Preparation time **15 minutes**
Cooking temperature **high**
Cooking time **1½–2 hours**
Serves **4**

40 g (1½ oz) **butter**
4 **spring onions**, sliced
1 **courgette**, about 200 g
  (7 oz), thinly sliced
100 g (3½ oz) podded fresh
  broad beans
6 **eggs**
250 ml (8 fl oz) **crème fraîche**
2 teaspoons chopped
  tarragon
2 tablespoons chopped
  parsley
salt and **pepper**

Preheat the slow cooker if necessary; see the manufacturer's instructions. Heat the butter, spring onions and courgette in a saucepan or in a bowl in the microwave until the butter has melted.

Line the slow cooker pot with nonstick baking paper, tip in the courgette and butter mix, then add the broad beans. Fork together the eggs, crème fraîche, herbs and a little salt and pepper in a bowl, then pour into the pot. Cover with the lid and cook on high for 1½–2 hours or until set in the middle.

Lift the pot out of the housing using oven gloves. Loosen the edge of the frittata with a knife, carefully turn out on to a large plate and peel off the lining paper. Cut the frittata into wedges and serve with salad and spoonfuls of Beetroot Chutney (see pages 214–215), if liked.

For courgette, salmon & asparagus frittata, add 100 g (3½ oz) sliced asparagus tips to the butter, onions and courgette when heating and replace the broad beans with 100 g (3½ oz) chopped smoked salmon. Continue as above.

chillied sweetcorn

Preparation time **15 minutes**
Cooking temperature **high**
Cooking time **2–3 hours**
Serves **4**

1 tablespoon **sunflower oil**
1 **onion**, finely chopped
1 **orange pepper**, cored,
    deseeded and diced
100 g (3½ oz) frozen
    sweetcorn, thawed
1 **garlic clove**, finely chopped
large pinch of **crushed dried
    red chillies**
½ teaspoon **ground cumin**
1 teaspoon **ground coriander**
410 g (13½ oz) can **mixed
    pulses**
400 g (13 oz) can **chopped
    tomatoes**
150 ml (¼ pint) **vegetable
    stock**
2 teaspoons **brown sugar**
salt and **pepper**

To serve
8 tablespoons **crème fraîche**
grated **Cheddar cheese**

Preheat the slow cooker if necessary; see the manufacturer's instructions. Heat the oil in a large frying pan, add the onion and fry for 5 minutes, stirring, until softened.

Stir in the pepper, sweetcorn, garlic and spices and cook for 1 minute. Add the pulses, tomatoes, stock, sugar and a little salt and pepper and bring to the boil.

Pour the mixture into the slow cooker pot, cover with the lid and cook on high for 2–3 hours or until cooked through. Spoon into bowls and serve with crème fraîche and cheese, or spoon on top of baked potatoes.

For chillied mushrooms, fry the onion as above then add 250 g (8 oz) quartered closed cup mushrooms instead of the pepper and sweetcorn, fry for 2–3 minutes, then add the garlic and spices and continue as above.

roasted vegetable terrine

Preparation time **30 minutes**,
   plus cooling
Cooking temperature **high**
Cooking time **2–3 hours**
Serves **4**

375 g (12 oz) **courgettes**,
   thinly sliced
1 **red pepper**, cored,
   deseeded and quartered
1 **orange pepper**, cored,
   deseeded and quartered
2 tablespoons **olive oil**, plus
   extra for greasing
1 **garlic clove**, finely chopped
2 **eggs**
150 ml (¼ pint) **milk**
25 g (1 oz) **Parmesan
   cheese**, grated
3 tablespoons chopped **basil**
salt and **pepper**

Preheat the slow cooker if necessary; see the manufacturer's instructions. Line the grill rack with foil. Arrange all the vegetables on the foil in a single layer, with the peppers skin side up. Drizzle with the oil and sprinkle with the garlic and salt and pepper. Grill for 10 minutes or until softened and browned. Transfer the courgette slices to a plate and wrap the peppers in the foil. Leave to stand for 5 minutes to loosen the skins.

Oil a 500 g (1 lb) loaf tin and line the base and two long sides with nonstick baking paper, checking first it will fit in the slow cooker pot. Beat together the eggs, milk, Parmesan, basil and salt and pepper in a bowl. Unwrap the peppers, peel away the skins with a knife.

Arrange one-third of the courgette slices over the base of the tin. Spoon in a little of the custard, then add the peppers and a little more custard. Repeat, ending with a layer of courgettes and custard. Cover the top with foil and put in the slow cooker pot. Pour boiling water into the pot to come halfway up the sides of the tin. Cover with the lid and cook on high for 2–3 hours or until the custard is set.

Lift out the tin using a tea towel and leave to cool. Loosen the edges with a knife, turn out on to a chopping board and peel off the lining paper. Cut into slices and serve with romseco sauce (see below).

For romesco sauce to accompany the terrine, fry 1 chopped onion in 1 tablespoon olive oil until softened. Mix in 2 chopped garlic cloves, 4 skinned and chopped tomatoes, ½ teaspoon paprika and 40 g (1½ oz) finely chopped almonds. Simmer for 10 minutes until thick.

irish stew

Preparation time **20 minutes**
Cooking temperature **high**
Cooking time **6–7 hours**
Serves **4**

2 tablespoons **sunflower oil**
1 kg (2 lb) **stewing lamb** or
  budget lamb chops of
  different sizes
1 **onion**, roughly chopped
3 **carrots**, sliced
250 g (8 oz) **swede**, diced
250 g (8 oz) **parsnips**, diced
2 tablespoons **plain flour**
400 g (13 oz) **potatoes**, cut
  into chunks no bigger than
  4 cm (1½ inch) square
800 ml (1 pint 7 fl oz) **lamb** or
  chicken stock
3 sprigs of **rosemary**
salt and **pepper**
4 tablespoons mixed chopped
  chives and **rosemary**, to
  garnish

Preheat the slow cooker if necessary; see the manufacturer's instructions. Heat the oil in a large frying pan, add the lamb and fry until browned on both sides. Scoop out of the pan with a slotted spoon and transfer to a plate.

Add the onion to the pan and fry for 5 minutes or until softened. Add the carrots, swede and parsnips and cook for 1–2 minutes, then stir in the flour. Add the potatoes, stock, rosemary and plenty of salt and pepper and bring to the boil, stirring.

Pour into the slow cooker pot, add the lamb and press below the surface of the liquid. Cover with the lid and cook on high for 6–7 hours or until the lamb is falling off the bones and the potatoes are tender.

Spoon into shallow bowls, removing the lamb bones if liked, and sprinkle with the chopped chives and rosemary. Serve with a spoon and fork and crusty bread.

For lamb stew with dumplings, make up the stew as above. About 35–50 minutes before the end of cooking, mix 150 g (5 oz) self-raising flour, 75 g (3 oz) vegetable suet, 2 teaspoons chopped rosemary leaves and a little salt and pepper in a bowl. Stir in 5–7 tablespoons water to make a soft but not sticky dough. Shape into 12 balls, add to the slow cooker pot, cover and cook on high for 30–45 minutes until well risen.

moroccan meatballs

Preparation time **30 minutes**
Cooking temperature **low**
Cooking time **6–8 hours**
Serves **4**

500 g (1 lb) **minced turkey**
100 g (3½ oz) drained canned
  green lentils
1 **egg yolk**
1 tablespoon **olive oil**
1 **onion**, sliced
2 **garlic cloves**, finely
  chopped
1 teaspoon **turmeric**
1 teaspoon **ground coriander**
½ teaspoon **ground cumin**
½ teaspoon **ground cinnamon**
2.5 cm (1 inch) **fresh root
  ginger**, peeled and finely
  chopped
400 g (13 oz) can **chopped
  tomatoes**
150 ml (¼ pint) **chicken stock**
salt and **pepper**

Preheat the slow cooker if necessary; see the
manufacturer's instructions. Mix together the minced
turkey, green lentils, a little salt and pepper and the egg
yolk in a bowl or food processor. Divide into 20 pieces,
then shape into small balls with wetted hands.

Heat the oil in a large frying pan, add the meatballs and
fry, stirring, until browned but not cooked through. Lift
out of the pan with a slotted spoon and put into the
slow cooker pot. Add the onion and fry until softened,
then stir in the garlic, spices and ginger and cook for
1 minute.

Stir in the tomatoes, stock and a little salt and pepper
and bring to the boil, stirring. Pour over the meatballs,
cover with the lid and cook on low for 6–8 hours or
until cooked through. Stir, then spoon on to couscous-
lined plates (see below).

For lemon couscous to accompany the meatballs,
put 200 g (7 oz) couscous into a bowl, pour over
450 ml (¾ pint) boiling water, the grated rind and
juice of 1 lemon, 2 tablespoons olive oil and some salt
and pepper. Cover and leave to stand for 5 minutes.
Fluff up with a fork and stir in a small bunch of
chopped coriander.

chicken & sage hotpot

Preparation time **30 minutes**
Cooking temperature **high**
Cooking time **4–5 hours**
Serves **4**

1 tablespoon **sunflower oil**
6 boneless, skinless **chicken thighs**, about 550 g (1 lb 2 oz), each cut into 3 pieces
1 **onion**, sliced
4 **smoked streaky bacon rashers**, diced
2 tablespoons **plain flour**
600 ml (1 pint) **chicken stock** or a mix of **stock** and **dry cider**
2–3 sprigs of **sage**
125 g (4 oz) **black pudding**, diced (optional)
200 g (7 oz) **carrots**, diced
200 g (7 oz) **swede**, diced
625 g (1¼ lb) **potatoes**, thinly sliced
25 g (1 oz) **butter**
salt and **pepper**

Preheat the slow cooker if necessary; see the manufacturer's instructions. Heat the oil in a large frying pan, add the chicken a few pieces at a time until all the meat is in the pan, then add the onion and bacon and fry, stirring, until the chicken is golden.

Stir in the flour, then gradually mix in the stock. Add the sage sprigs and a little salt and pepper and bring to the boil, stirring. Add the black pudding, if using, carrots and swede to the slow cooker pot.

Pour over the hot chicken mixture, then arrange the potatoes overlapping on the top and press below the surface of the liquid. Sprinkle with a little extra salt and pepper, then cover with the lid and cook on high for 4–5 hours or until the potatoes are tender and the chicken is cooked through.

Lift the pot out of the housing using oven gloves, dot the potatoes with butter and brown under a hot grill. Spoon into shallow dishes to serve.

For mustardy beef hotpot, replace the chicken with 750 g (1½ lb) trimmed and diced stewing beef. Fry the beef in the oil and transfer to the slow cooker pot, then fry the onion, omitting the bacon. Stir in the flour, then mix in 600 ml (1 pint) beef stock, 2 teaspoons English mustard, 1 tablespoon Worcestershire sauce, 1 tablespoon tomato purée and salt and pepper and bring to the boil. Omit the black pudding and continue as above.

baked mackerel with beetroot

Preparation time **20 minutes**
Cooking temperature **high**
Cooking time **1½–2 hours**
Serves **4**

2 tablespoons **olive oil**
1 **onion**, sliced
1 **celery stick**, sliced
1 **carrot**, thinly sliced
2 tablespoons **light muscovado sugar**
4 tablespoons **cider vinegar**
200 ml (7 fl oz) **fish stock**
2 **bay leaves**
4 **cloves**
250 g (8 oz) pack **beetroot** in natural juice, drained and sliced
1 **dessert apple**, peeled, cored and sliced
4 **mackerel**, each about 200 g (7 oz), gutted, heads removed and rinsed in cold water

Mustard cream
2 teaspoons **wholegrain mustard**
6 tablespoons **crème fraîche**
2 tablespoons chopped **chives**, plus extra to garnish
salt and **pepper**

Preheat the slow cooker if necessary; see the manufacturer's instructions. Heat the oil in a frying pan, add the onion, celery and carrot and fry for about 5 minutes or until softened.

Add the sugar, vinegar, fish stock, bay leaves, cloves and a little salt and pepper and bring to the boil. Arrange the beetroot in the base of the slow cooker pot, then top with the apples. Slash the fish two or three times on each side, then arrange in a single layer on top of the apples.

Pour over the hot stock and vegetables, cover with the lid and cook on high for 1½–2 hours or until the fish flakes easily when pressed in the centre with a knife.

When almost ready to serve, mix together the ingredients for the mustard cream in a small bowl. Carefully transfer the fish, vegetables and some of the stock to shallow bowls, then garnish with chives. Serve with spoonfuls of the mustard cream and crusty sliced bread.

For baked mackerel with hot potato salad, make up the recipe as above, omitting the beetroot. When the fish is almost ready, cook 400 g (13 oz) baby new potatoes in a saucepan of boiling water for 15 minutes or until just tender. Make the mustard cream as above and toss with the hot potatoes. Serve with drained mackerel and sliced pickled cucumbers.

turkey & sausage stew

Preparation time **30 minutes**
Cooking temperature **high**
Cooking time **5½–6¾ hours**
Serves **4**

1 **turkey drumstick**, about
   700 g (1 lb 6 oz)
2 tablespoons **sunflower oil**
4 **smoked streaky bacon
   rashers**, diced
3 large **pork and herb
   sausages**, about 200 g
   (7 oz) in total, each cut into
   4 pieces
1 **onion**, sliced
1 **leek**, sliced; white and
   green parts kept separate
2 tablespoons **plain flour**
600 ml (1 pint) **chicken stock**
small bunch of **mixed herbs**
300 g (10 oz) **baby carrots**,
   halved if large
2 **celery sticks**, sliced
65 g (2½ oz) fresh **cranberries**
salt and **pepper**

Parsley dumplings
150 g (5 oz) **self-raising flour**
75 g (3 oz) **shredded suet**
4 tablespoons chopped
   parsley
5–7 tablespoons **water**

Preheat the slow cooker if necessary; see the manufacturer's instructions. If the turkey drumstick does not fit into the slow cooker pot sever the knuckle end with a large heavy knife, hitting it with a rolling pin.

Heat the oil in a large frying pan, add the drumstick, bacon and sausage pieces and fry, turning until browned all over. Transfer to the slow cooker pot. Add the onion and white leeks slices to the pan and fry until softened. Stir in the flour, then mix in the stock. Add the herbs, salt and pepper and bring to the boil.

Add the carrots, celery and cranberries to the pot and pour over the hot onion mixture. Cover with the lid and cook on high for 5–6 hours or until the turkey is almost falling off the bone. Lift the turkey out of the slow cooker pot. Remove and discard the skin, then cut the meat into pieces, discarding the bones and tendons. Return meat to the pot with the reserved green leek slices.

Make the dumplings. Mix the flour, suet, parsley and salt and pepper in a bowl. Stir in enough water to make a soft dough. Knead, then shape into 12 small balls. Arrange over the turkey, replace the lid and cook, still on high, for 30–45 minutes or until the dumplings are cooked through. Spoon into shallow bowls to serve.

For turkey & cranberry puff pie, make the stew as above. Roll out 500 g (1 lb) puff pastry, trim to an oval a little larger than the top of the slow cooker pot and put on an oiled baking sheet. Brush the top with beaten egg, then bake in a preheated oven at 200°C (400°F), Gas Mark 6 for about 25 minutes until golden. Spoon the stew on to plates and top with wedges of the pastry.

indian spiced cottage pie

Preparation time **30 minutes**
Cooking temperature **low**
Cooking time **8–10 hours**
Serves **4**

1 tablespoon **sunflower oil**
500 g (1 lb) lean **minced beef**
1 **onion**, chopped
4 tablespoons **korma curry paste**
1 teaspoon **turmeric**
2 **carrots**, diced
2 tablespoons **plain flour**
100 g (3½ oz) **red lentils**
50 g (2 oz) **sultanas**
1 tablespoon **tomato purée**
900 ml (1½ pints) **beef stock**
salt and **pepper**

Topping
875 g (1¾ lb) **potatoes**, cut into chunks
50 g (2 oz) **butter**
3 tablespoons **milk**
1 tablespoon **sunflower oil**
1 bunch of **spring onions**, chopped
½ teaspoon **turmeric**

Preheat the slow cooker if necessary; see the manufacturer's instructions. Heat the oil in a large frying pan, add the beef and onion, breaking up and stirring the meat until it is evenly browned. Stir in the curry paste and turmeric and cook for 1 minute. Stir in the carrots and flour, then add the lentils, sultanas, tomato purée, stock and salt and pepper. Bring to the boil, stirring, then pour into the slow cooker pot. Cover with the lid and cook on low for 8–10 hours or until the lentils are soft and the beef is tender.

When almost ready to serve, put the potatoes in a saucepan of boiling water and simmer for 15 minutes or until tender. Drain and mash with half the butter, milk and salt and pepper. Heat the oil in a frying pan, add the spring onions and fry for 2–3 minutes or until softened. Add the turmeric and cook for 1 minute, then mix into the mash.

Stir the beef mixture and lift the pot out of the housing using oven gloves. Transfer to a serving dish if liked. Spoon the mash on top, dot with remaining butter, then grill until golden. Serve with cooked peas.

For traditional cottage pie, fry the beef and onion as above. Omit the curry paste and turmeric. Add the carrots and flour, then replace the lentils and sultanas with a 400 g (13 oz) can baked beans, 1 tablespoon tomato purée, 1 tablespoon Worcestershire sauce, 300 ml (½ pint) beef stock and 1 teaspoon dried mixed herbs. Transfer to the slow cooker pot and continue as above. Top with the mash, omitting the spring onions and turmeric. Spoon over the mince, sprinkle with 50 g (2 oz) grated Cheddar cheese and grill.

sausage tagliatelle

Preparation time **25 minutes**
Cooking temperature **low**
Cooking time **8–10 hours**
Serves **4**

1 tablespoon **sunflower oil**
8 **chilli** or **spicy sausages**
1 **onion**, chopped
150 g (5 oz) **cup mushrooms**, sliced
2 **garlic cloves**, finely chopped
400 g (13 oz) can **chopped tomatoes**
150 ml (¼ pint) **beef stock**
250 g (8 oz) **tagliatelle**
salt and **pepper**

To serve
basil leaves
freshly grated **Parmesan cheese** (optional)

Preheat the slow cooker if necessary; see the manufacturer's instructions. Heat the oil in a large frying pan, add the sausages and fry, turning until browned but not cooked through. Transfer to the slow cooker pot with tongs.

Drain off the excess fat from the pan to leave 2 teaspoons, then add the onion and fry until softened. Mix in the mushrooms and garlic and fry for a 1–2 minutes.

Stir in the chopped tomatoes, stock and a little salt and pepper and bring to the boil, stirring. Pour the mixture over the sausages, cover with the lid and cook on low for 8–10 hours or until cooked through.

When almost ready to serve, bring a large saucepan of water to the boil, add the tagliatelle and cook for 7–8 minutes or until just tender then drain. Lift the sausages out of the slow cooker pot and slice thickly, then return to the pot with the pasta and mix together. Sprinkle with torn basil leaves and grated Parmesan, if liked. Serve with a green salad.

For chicken & chorizo tagliatelle, omit the sausages and fry 500 g (1 lb) diced boneless chicken thighs in 1 tablespoon olive oil until golden. Drain and transfer to the slow cooker pot. Continue as above, adding 100 g (3½ oz) diced chorizo sausage to the frying pan with the onions and replacing the beef stock with 150 ml (¼ pint) chicken stock.

chicken & haricot bean stew

Preparation time **20 minutes**
Cooking temperature **low**
Cooking time **8–9 hours**
Serves **4**

2 tablespoons **olive oil**
625 g (1¼ lb) boneless,
   skinless **chicken thighs**,
   cubed
1 **onion**, sliced
2 **garlic cloves**, finely
   chopped
2 tablespoons **plain flour**
600 ml (1 pint) **chicken stock**
1 **red pepper**, cored,
   deseeded and sliced
198 g (7 oz) can **sweetcorn**,
   drained
410 g (13½ oz) can **haricot
   beans**, drained
300 g (10 oz) small **new
   potatoes**, scrubbed and
   thinly sliced
2 sprigs of **thyme**, plus extra
   to garnish (optional)
salt and **pepper**

Preheat the slow cooker if necessary; see the manufacturer's instructions. Heat the oil in a large frying pan, add the chicken and onion and fry, stirring, until lightly browned.

Stir in the garlic and flour, then gradually mix in the stock. Add the red pepper, sweetcorn, haricot beans and new potatoes. Add the thyme and a little salt and pepper and bring to the boil, stirring.

Transfer the mixture to the slow cooker pot and press the chicken and potatoes below the surface of the liquid. Cover with the lid and cook on low for 8–9 hours or until the chicken is cooked through and the potatoes are tender.

Stir well, then spoon into shallow bowls and sprinkle with a few extra thyme leaves, if liked. Serve with hot garlic bread.

For Spanish chicken with chorizo, fry the chicken and onion with 75 g (3 oz) ready-diced chorizo until well coloured, then mix in 1 teaspoon smoked paprika, the garlic and flour. Continue as above, replacing the thyme with 2 rosemary sprigs. Serve sprinkled with chopped parsley.

bacon & leek suet pudding

Preparation time **30 minutes**
Cooking temperature **high**
Cooking time **4–5 hours**
Serves **4**

25 g (1 oz) **butter**
2 **smoked gammon steaks**,
   about 450 g (14½ oz) in
   total, diced and any fat and
   rind discarded
250 g (8 oz) **leeks**, trimmed,
   cleaned and sliced
300 g (10 oz) **self-raising
   flour**
150 g (5 oz) **vegetable suet**
3 teaspoons dry **mustard
   powder**
200–250 ml (7–8 fl oz) **water**
salt and **pepper**

Parsley sauce
25 g (1 oz) **butter**
25 g (1 oz) **plain flour**
300 ml (½ pint) **milk**
20 g (¾ oz) **parsley**, finely
   chopped

Preheat the slow cooker if necessary; see the manufacturer's instructions. Heat the butter in a frying pan, add the gammon and leeks and fry, stirring, for 4–5 minutes or until the leeks have just softened. Season with pepper only. Leave to cool slightly.

Put the flour, ½ teaspoon salt, a large pinch of pepper, the suet and mustard powder in a bowl and mix well. Gradually stir in enough water to make a soft but not sticky dough. Knead lightly, then roll out on a large piece of floured nonstick baking paper to a rectangle 23 x 30 cm (9 x 12 inches). Turn the paper so that the shorter edges are facing you.

Spoon the gammon mixture over the pastry, leaving 2 cm (¾ inch) around the edges. Roll up, starting at the shorter edge, using the paper to help. Wrap in the paper, then in a sheet of foil. Twist the ends together tightly, leaving some space for the pudding to rise.

Transfer the pudding to the slow cooker pot and raise off the base slightly by standing it on 2 ramekin dishes. Pour boiling water into the pot to come a little up the sides of the pudding, being careful that the water cannot seep through any joins. Cover with the lid and cook on high for 4–5 hours or until the pudding is well risen.

Just before serving, melt the butter for the sauce in a saucepan. Stir in the flour, then gradually mix in the milk and bring to the boil, stirring until smooth. Cook for 1–2 minutes, then stir in the parsley and season. Lift the pudding out of the slow cooker pot, unwrap and cut into slices. Arrange on plates and spoon over a little sauce. Serve with sugar snap peas.

short-cut suppers

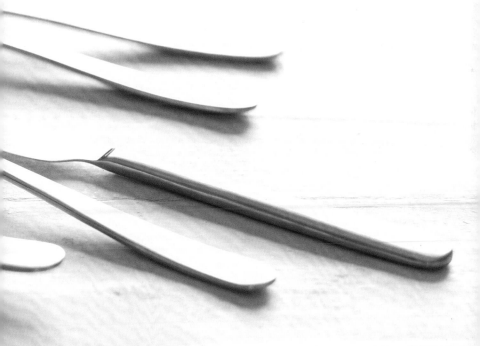

chicken & sweet potato balti

Preparation time **15 minutes**
Cooking temperature **high** and
  low
Cooking time **6–7 hours**
Serves **4**

6 boneless, skinless **chicken
  thighs**, about 500 g (1 lb)
  in total, cubed
1 **onion**, sliced
375 g (12 oz) **sweet
  potatoes**, cut into 2 cm
  (¾ inch) cubes
2 **garlic cloves**, finely
  chopped
425 g (14 oz) jar **balti curry
  sauce**
chopped **coriander**, to garnish
  (optional)

Preheat the slow cooker if necessary; see the manufacturer's instructions. Arrange the chicken, onion and sweet potatoes in the base of the slow cooker pot in an even layer. Sprinkle with the garlic.

Bring the curry sauce just to the boil in a small saucepan or the microwave. Pour into the slow cooker pot in an even layer. Cover with the lid and cook on high for 30 minutes. Reduce the heat and cook on low for 5½–6½ hours, or set to auto for 6–7 hours, until the chicken is cooked through and the sauce piping hot.

Stir well, then sprinkle with roughly chopped coriander, if liked. Spoon into bowls and serve with warmed naan bread.

For harissa baked chicken with sweet potato,
prepare the chicken and vegetables as above. Replace the balti curry sauce with 400 g (13 oz) can chopped tomatoes and 2 teaspoons harissa paste. Continue as above.

balsamic braised pork chops

Preparation time **15 minutes**
Cooking temperature **high** and
  low
Cooking time **7–8 hours**
Serves **4**

4 **spare rib pork chops**,
  about 750 g (1 ½ lb) in total
3 tablespoons **apple**
  balsamic or **plain balsamic**
  vinegar
2 tablespoons **light**
  muscovado sugar
2 **onions**, thinly sliced
2 **dessert apples**, peeled,
  cored and quartered
2 tablespoons **cornflour**
3 teaspoons **English mustard**
200 ml (7 fl oz) boiling
  chicken stock
chopped **chives**, to garnish
  (optional)

Preheat the slow cooker if necessary; see the manufacturer's instructions. Put the pork chops into the base of the slow cooker pot and spoon over the vinegar and sugar. Sprinkle the onions on top, then add the apples.

Put the cornflour and mustard in a small bowl and mix with a little cold water to make a smooth paste, then gradually stir in the boiling stock until smooth. Pour over the pork. Cover with the lid and cook on high for 30 minutes. Reduce the heat and cook on low for 6½–7½ hours, or set to auto for 7–8 hours, until the pork is cooked through and tender.

Transfer the pork to serving plates, stir the sauce and spoon over the chops. Sprinkle with chopped chives, if liked, and serve with mash and Brussel sprouts.

For cider-braised pork, prepare the pork chops as above, omitting the vinegar. Bring 200 ml (7 fl oz) dry cider to the boil in a saucepan. Make up the cornflour paste as above, then gradually stir in the boiling cider instead of the stock. Pour over the chops and continue as above.

baked seafood with saffron

Preparation time **15 minutes**
Cooking temperature **low** and
  high
Cooking time **5½–7½ hours**
Serves **4**

1 **onion**, finely chopped
1 **red pepper**, cored,
  deseeded and diced
2 **garlic cloves**, finely
  chopped
400 g (13 oz) can **chopped
  tomatoes**
150 ml (¼ pint) **dry white
  wine** or **fish stock**
large pinch of **saffron threads**
2 sprigs of **thyme**
1 tablespoon **olive oil**
400 g (13 oz) pack frozen
  seafood (prawns, mussels,
  squid), thawed
300 g (10 oz) **tagliatelle**
salt and **pepper**
chopped **parsley**, to garnish

Preheat the slow cooker if necessary; see the manufacturer's instructions. Put the onion, red pepper, garlic and tomatoes into the slow cooker pot, then add the wine or stock, saffron, thyme, oil and a little salt and pepper.

Cover with the lid and cook on low for 5–7 hours. Rinse the seafood with cold water, drain and then stir into the slow cooker pot. Replace the lid and cook on high for 30 minutes or until piping hot.

When almost ready to serve, bring a large saucepan of water to the boil, add the pasta and cook for 8–10 minutes or until just tender. Drain and toss with the parsley. Spoon into shallow bowls and top with the seafood sauce.

For baked salmon with pesto, omit the seafood and drain a 400 g (13 oz) can red salmon, remove the skin and bones and break the fish into large flakes. Put the onion, red pepper and garlic into the slow cooker pot. Heat the tomatoes and wine or stock in a small saucepan or the microwave, then add to the pot with 2 teaspoons pesto and the oil, omitting the saffron and thyme. Mix in the salmon and continue as above.

pot roast lamb with rosemary

Preparation time **5 minutes**
Cooking temperature **high**
Cooking time **7–8 hours**
Serves **4**

1–1.2 kg (2–2 lb 7 oz) **half
   lamb shoulder on the bone**
3 sprigs of **rosemary**
1 **red onion**, cut into wedges
2 tablespoons **redcurrant jelly**
250 ml (8 fl oz) **red wine**
250 ml (8 fl oz) **lamb stock**
salt and **pepper**

Preheat the slow cooker if necessary; see the manufacturer's instructions. Put the lamb into the slow cooker pot, add the rosemary on top and tuck the onion wedges around the sides of the joint.

Spoon the redcurrant jelly into a small saucepan and add the wine, stock and a little salt and pepper. Bring to the boil, stirring so that the jelly melts, then pour over the lamb. Cover with the lid and cook on high for 7–8 hours or until a knife goes into the centre of the lamb easily and the meat is almost falling off the bone.

Lift the joint out of the slow cooker pot and put it on to a serving plate with the onions. Discard the rosemary sprigs and pour the wine and stock mixture into a jug to serve as gravy. Carve the lamb on to plates and serve with steamed green vegetables and baby potatoes or crushed new potatoes with rosemary cream (see below).

For crushed new potatoes with rosemary cream to accompany the lamb, bring a pan of water to the boil, add 500 g (1 lb) baby new potatoes and cook for 15 minutes. Add 200 g (7 oz) tenderstem broccoli, thickly sliced, for the last 5 minutes. Drain and then roughly break up with a fork. Stir in 1 tablespoon finely chopped rosemary, 4 tablespoons crème fraîche and a little salt and pepper. Spoon a mound of potatoes into the centre of 4 serving plates, then top with the carved pot roast lamb and drizzle the gravy around the edges of the mash.

honey-glazed gammon

Preparation time **20 minutes**, plus overnight soaking
Cooking temperature **high**
Cooking time **5–7 hours**
Serves **4**

1 kg (2 lb) boneless **smoked gammon** joint, soaked overnight in cold water
1 **onion**, cut into wedges
300 g (10 oz) **carrots**, halved lengthways and cut into 2.5 cm (1 inch) chunks
500 g (1 lb) medium **baking potatoes**, scrubbed and quartered
2 **bay leaves**
6 **cloves**
½ teaspoon **black peppercorns**
900 ml (1½ pints) boiling **water**

Glaze
2 tablespoons **runny honey**
2 teaspoons **English mustard**

Preheat the slow cooker if necessary; see the manufacturer's instructions. Put the gammon joint into the slow cooker pot. Tuck the vegetables around the sides, then add the bay leaves, cloves and peppercorns. Pour over the boiling water to just cover the gammon.

Cover with the lid and cook on high for 5–7 hours or until the gammon and vegetables are cooked through and tender. Lift the gammon out of the slow cooker pot and transfer to the base of a grill pan. Cut away the rind and discard.

Mix the honey and mustard together for the glaze, spoon over the top and sides of the joint, then add 3 ladlefuls of stock from the slow cooker pot to the base of the grill pan. Grill until the gammon is golden brown. Carve into slices and serve with the sauce from the grill pan and drained vegetables from the slow cooker pot. Accompany with steamed green beans, if liked.

For glazed gammon with pease pudding, soak 200 g (7 oz) dried yellow split peas in cold water overnight while soaking the gammon in a separate bowl of cold water. Next day, drain the peas, add to a saucepan with 1.2 litres (2 pints) water, bring to the boil and boil rapidly for 10 minutes. Add the gammon joint, onion, carrots, bay leaves, cloves and peppercorns to the slow cooker pot, omitting the potatoes. Pour in the hot peas and their water, then continue as above. When the glazed gammon is grilled, drain off most of the stock from the peas and carrots, then mash and stir in 25 g (1 oz) butter and a little salt, if needed. Serve the pease pudding with the sliced gammon.

keema mutter

Preparation time **10 minutes**
Cooking temperature **high** and
low
Cooking time **8–10 hours**
Serves **4**

500 g (1 lb) **lean minced
beef**
1 **onion**, finely chopped
400 g (13 oz) can **chopped
tomatoes**
3 tablespoons **mild curry
paste**
2 teaspoons **cumin seeds**
2–3 **bird's eye green chillies**,
deseeded and sliced
2.5 cm (1 inch) **fresh root
ginger**, peeled and finely
chopped
2 **garlic cloves**, finely
chopped
50 g (2 oz) **creamed
coconut**, crumbled
125 ml (4 fl oz) boiling **beef
stock**
150 g (5 oz) frozen **peas**
chopped **coriander** and extra
sliced **chillies**, to garnish

Preheat the slow cooker if necessary; see the
manufacturer's instructions. Put the beef, onion and
tomatoes into the slow cooker pot, then stir in the curry
paste, cumin seeds, chilli, ginger and garlic. Sprinkle the
coconut over the top, then stir in the boiling stock.

Cover with the lid and cook on high for 30 minutes.
Reduce the heat and cook on low for 7–9 hours, or set
to auto for 7½–9½ hours Stir the minced beef well to
break up into small pieces, then mix in the peas and
cook on high for 30 minutes or until cooked through.

When almost ready to serve, sprinkle with the chopped
coriander and sliced chillies. Serve with warmed
chapattis and a tomato and red onion salad.

For keema aloo, make up the recipe as above,
replacing the minced beef with 500 g (1 lb) minced
lamb. Stir in 200 g (7 oz) potatoes, cut into small dice,
after adding the garlic. At the end of cooking, replace
the peas with 125 g (4 oz) washed, torn spinach.
Serve sprinkled with 4 finely sliced spring onions and
a little chopped coriander.

tomato braised squid with chorizo

Preparation time **20 minutes**
Cooking temperature **low**
Cooking time **3½–5½ hours**
Serves **4**

625 g (1¼ lb) chilled **squid**
1 **onion**, thinly sliced
125 g (4 oz) ready-diced
  chorizo
125 g (4 oz) **cup
  mushrooms**, sliced
1 **red pepper**, cored,
  deseeded and sliced
2 **garlic cloves**, finely
  chopped
2–3 sprigs of **rosemary**,
  leaves stripped from the
  stems
1 tablespoon **tomato purée**
1 teaspoon **caster sugar**
400 g (13 oz) can **chopped
  tomatoes**
100 ml (3½ fl oz) **red wine**
1 tablespoon **cornflour**
salt and **pepper**
chopped **parsley**, to garnish

Preheat the slow cooker if necessary; see the manufacturer's instructions. Rinse the squid inside and out, pulling off the tentacles and reserving. Drain and slice the bodies. Put the tentacles in a bowl, cover with clingfilm and chill in the refrigerator.

Put the onion, chorizo, mushrooms and red pepper into the slow cooker pot. Add the garlic, rosemary, tomato purée and sugar, then stir in the sliced squid.

Pour the tomatoes and wine into a saucepan and bring to the boil or heat in the microwave. Add a little salt and pepper, then pour into the slow cooker pot and stir well. Cover with the lid and cook on low for 3–5 hours or until the squid is tender.

When almost ready to serve, put the cornflour in a small bowl with a little cold water and mix to a smooth paste. Stir into the slow cooker pot, add the squid tentacles, then replace the lid and cook, still on low, for 30 minutes. Spoon into bowls and sprinkle with chopped parsley. Serve with thickly sliced bread or rice.

For tomato-braised squid with red onion, replace the onion, mushrooms and chorizo with 2 large thinly sliced red onions and put in the slow cooker pot with the red pepper, garlic, tomato purée and sugar, adding 2 bay leaves instead of the rosemary. Add the squid and continue as above.

hot spanish beans

Preparation time **10 minutes**
Cooking temperature **high**
Cooking time **4–5 hours**
Serves **4**

125 g (4 oz) **chorizo**, sliced
1 **red onion**, chopped
2 x 410 g (13½ oz) cans
   haricot beans, drained
375 g (12 oz) **cherry
   tomatoes**
2 **garlic cloves**, finely
   chopped
2–3 sprigs of **rosemary**,
   leaves stripped from the
   stems
350 g (11½ oz) pack chilled
   frankfurters, drained and
   thickly sliced
100 g (3½ oz) marinated
   mixed olives (optional)
200 ml (7 fl oz) boiling
   vegetable stock
1 tablespoon **tomato purée**
salt and **pepper**

Preheat the slow cooker if necessary; see the manufacturer's instructions. Put the chorizo, onion and haricot beans into the slow cooker pot, add the tomatoes, garlic and rosemary and mix together. Arrange the frankfurters and olives, if using, on the top.

Mix the boiling stock with the tomato purée and a little salt and pepper, then pour into the slow cooker pot. Cover with the lid and cook on high for 4–5 hours. Stir the beans, then spoon into bowls. Serve with hot peppered foccacia or garlic bread and a green leafy salad.

For mustard beans, put the onion, beans, tomatoes and garlic in the slow cooker pot, omitting the chorizo, rosemary and olives. Add 1 cored, deseeded and diced red pepper. Mix the stock with 2 tablespoons tomato purée, 2 tablespoons Worcestershire sauce, 1 tablespoon Dijon mustard, ½ teaspoon smoked paprika and salt and pepper. Pour over the beans and add the frankfurters. Continue as above.

pork with black bean sauce

Preparation time **20 minutes**, plus overnight marinating
Cooking temperature **high and low**
Cooking time **8–10 hours**
Serves **4**

4 **spare rib pork steaks**, about 175 g (6 oz) each
2 tablespoons **cornflour**
4 tablespoons **soy sauce**
4 cm (1½ inches) **fresh root ginger**, peeled and finely chopped
2 **garlic cloves**, finely chopped
100 g (3½ oz) **black bean sauce**
300 ml (½ pint) boiling **chicken stock**
pepper

To serve
1 tablespoon **sunflower oil**
300 g (10 oz) **mixed vegetable stir-fry**
cooked **rice**

Put the pork steaks into a shallow non-metallic dish. Put the cornflour and soy sauce in a small bowl and mix to a smooth paste, then add the ginger, garlic, black bean sauce and a little pepper. Pour over the pork, cover with clingfilm and marinate in the refrigerator overnight.

Preheat the slow cooker if necessary; see the manufacturer's instructions. Put the pork and marinade into the slow cooker pot. Pour over the boiling stock, cover with the lid and cook on high for 30 minutes. Reduce the heat and cook on low for 7½–9½ hours, or set to auto for 8–10 hours, until the pork is cooked through and tender.

When almost ready to serve, heat the oil in a large frying pan, add the mixed vegetables and stir-fry for 2–3 minutes or until just tender. Spoon the pork on to plates lined with rice and top with the vegetables.

For sweet & sour pork, omit the black bean sauce from the marinade, add the marinated pork to the slow cooker pot with 1 bunch of sliced spring onions, 1 cored, deseeded and sliced red pepper and 100 g (3½ oz) sliced mushrooms. Replace the chicken stock with a 425 g (14 oz) jar sweet and sour sauce. Bring the sauce to the boil in a saucepan or the microwave, then pour into the slow cooker pot. Continue as above.

fragrant spiced chicken with chilli

Preparation time **15 minutes**
Cooking temperature **high**
Cooking time **5–6 hours**
Serves **4–5**

1.5 kg (3 lb) oven-ready whole
  chicken, rinsed with cold
  water, drained well
1 **onion**, chopped
200 g (7 oz) **carrots**, sliced
7.5 cm (3 inches) **fresh root
  ginger**, peeled and sliced
2 **garlic cloves**, sliced
1 large **mild red chilli**, halved
3 large **star anise**
4 tablespoons **soy sauce**
4 tablespoons **rice vinegar**
1 tablespoon **light
  muscovado sugar**
900 ml (1½ pints) boiling
  water
small bunch of **coriander**
200 g (7 oz) dried **egg
  noodles**
75 g (3 oz) **mangetout**, thickly
  sliced
2 **pak choi**, about 150 g
  (5 oz), thickly sliced
salt and **pepper**

Preheat the slow cooker if necessary; see the manufacturer's instructions. Put chicken breast side down into the slow cooker pot. Add the onion, carrots, ginger, garlic, chilli and star anise and spoon over the soy sauce, vinegar and sugar.

Pour over the boiling water. Cut the coriander leaves from the stems; add the stems to the pot, reserving the leaves. Season, cover with the lid and cook on high for 5–6 hours or until the juices run clear when the thickest part of the leg is pierced with a knife.

When almost ready to serve, put the noodles into a large bowl, cover with boiling water and leave to soak for 5 minutes. Lift the chicken out of the slow cooker pot, put on to a plate, cover with foil and keep hot. Add the mangetout and pak choi to the pot, replace the lid and cook, still on high, for 5–10 minutes or until just wilted.

Carve the chicken into bite-sized pieces. Drain the noodles, divide between 4 bowls. Top with chicken and chopped coriander leaves, then ladle over the hot broth.

For Italian spiced chicken with pesto, put the chicken into the pot with the onion, carrot and garlic only and add 1 sliced fennel bulb and 1 sliced lemon. Continue as above, replacing the coriander with basil. When the chicken is removed, add the mangetout, 3 chopped tomatoes, 150 g (5 oz) chopped purple sprouting broccoli and 2 tablespoons pesto sauce, cover and cook for 5–10 minutes. Omit the pak choi. Put a 250 g (8 oz) pack fresh tagliatelle in a saucepan of boiling water and cook for 2 minutes. Drain and continue as above.

smoked cod with bean mash

Preparation time **15 minutes**
Cooking temperature **low**
Cooking time **1½–2 hours**
Serves **4**

2 x 410 g (13½ oz) cans
  cannellini beans, drained
bunch of **spring onions**, thinly
  sliced; white and green parts
  kept separate
400 ml (14 fl oz) boiling **fish
  stock**
1 teaspoon **wholegrain
  mustard**
grated rind and juice of
  1 **lemon**
4 **smoked cod loins**, about
  625 g (1¼ lb) in total
4 tablespoons **crème fraîche**
small bunch of **parsley**,
  watercress or **rocket
  leaves**, roughly chopped
salt and **pepper**

Preheat the slow cooker if necessary; see the manufacturer's instructions. Put the drained beans into the slow cooker pot with the white onion slices. Mix the fish stock with the mustard, lemon rind and juice and a little salt and pepper, then pour into the pot.

Arrange the fish on top and sprinkle with a little extra pepper. Cover with the lid and cook on low for 1½–2 hours or until the fish flakes easily when pressed in the centre with a knife.

Lift out the fish with a fish slice and transfer to a plate. Pour off nearly all the cooking liquid, then mash the beans roughly. Stir in the crème fraîche, the remaining onion and the parsley, watercress or rocket. Taste and adjust the seasoning, if needed. Spoon the mash on to plates and top with the fish.

For baked salmon with basil bean mash, add the beans to the slow cooker pot with the ingredients as above, omitting the mustard. Arrange 4 x 150 g (5 oz) salmon steaks on top, season and cook as above. Mash the beans with the crème fraîche, green spring onions and a small bunch of roughly torn basil and serve with the fish as above.

asian glazed ribs

Preparation time **25 minutes**, plus overnight marinating

Cooking temperature **high and low**

Cooking time **8–10 hours**, plus 10–15 minutes grilling

Serves **4**

1 **onion**, quartered

5 cm (2 inches) **fresh root ginger**, peeled and sliced

2 tablespoons **rice or white wine vinegar**

4 **star anise**

1 **cinnamon stick**, halved

1.25 kg (2½ lb) **pork ribs**

1 litre (1¾ pints) boiling **water**

2 **breakfast tea bags**

Glaze

4 tablespoons **runny honey**

4 tablespoons **soy sauce**

Put the onion, ginger, vinegar, star anise and cinnamon into a bowl and cover with clingfilm. Chill in the refrigerator overnight.

Preheat the slow cooker if necessary; see the manufacturer's instructions. Pour the boiling water over the teabags and leave to brew for 2–3 minutes, then squeeze out the bags and discard. Rinse the ribs with cold water, drain and put into the slow cooker pot with the spiced onion mix and the hot tea.

Cover with the lid and cook on high for 30 minutes. Reduce the heat and cook on low for 7½–9½ hours, or set to auto for 8–10 hours, until the meat is almost falling off the bones.

Lift the ribs out of the slow cooker pot and transfer to a foil-lined grill pan. Put 6 tablespoons of stock from the pot into a bowl and mix in the honey and soy sauce. Spoon over the ribs, then grill for 10–15 minutes, turning several times and spooning soy mixture over until browned and glazed. Serve with pickled cucumber (see below) and rice.

For pickled cucumber to accompany the ribs, mix ¼–½ mild red chilli, deseeded and finely chopped, 3 tablespoons chopped coriander, 1 tablespoon rice or white wine vinegar, 1 teaspoon fish sauce and ½ teaspoon caster sugar in a salad bowl. Very thinly slice ½ cucumber, add to the dressing and toss together gently. This dish can be made, covered with clingfilm and kept in the refrigerator overnight.

stifado

Preparation time **25 minutes**, plus overnight marinating
Cooking temperature **high and low**
Cooking time **10–11 hours**
Serves **4**

200 ml (7 fl oz) **red wine**
1 tablespoon **tomato purée**
2 tablespoons **olive oil**
2–3 sprigs of **thyme** or **bay leaves**
4 **cloves**
¼ teaspoon **ground allspice**
300 g (10 oz) **shallots**, halved if large
2 **garlic cloves**, finely chopped
750 g (1½ lb) **stewing beef**, cut into large chunks and any fat discarded
4 teaspoons **cornflour**
150 ml (¼ pint) cold **water**
½ **stock cube**
salt and **pepper**

Mix the wine, tomato purée and oil in a shallow non-metallic dish. Add the herbs, spices and a little salt and pepper and mix together. Mix in the shallots and garlic, then add the beef and toss in the marinade. Cover with clingfilm and marinate in the refrigerator overnight.

Preheat the slow cooker if necessary; see the manufacturer's instructions. Put the cornflour into a saucepan, mix in a little of the water to make a smooth paste, then mix in the remaining water. Drain the marinade from the beef into the pan and crumble in the stock cube. Bring to the boil, stirring

Tip the beef, shallots and flavourings into the slow cooker pot and pour over the hot stock. Cover with the lid and cook on high for 30 minutes. Reduce the heat and cook on low for 9½-10½ hours, or set to auto for 10–11 hours, until the meat is cooked through and tender. Spoon into bowls and serve with toasted French bread and herb butter.

For lamb stifado, mix together 200 ml (7 fl oz) white wine, 1 tablespoon tomato purée, 2 tablespoons olive oil, 2 bay leaves, 2 teaspoons roughly crushed coriander seeds and ½ sliced lemon, add the shallots and garlic and stir in 750 g (1½ lb) diced lamb shoulder or leg. Marinate overnight, then continue as above.

chicken avgolemono

Preparation time **30 minutes**
Cooking temperature **high** and
  low
Cooking time **6–8 hours**
Serves **4**

8 boneless, skinless **chicken
  thighs**, about 700 g (1 lb
  6 oz) in total, each cut into
  3 or 4 pieces
1 **onion**, thinly sliced
2–3 sprigs of **oregano** or
  basil
450 ml (¾ pint) boiling
  chicken stock
grated rind and juice of
  1 **lemon**
300 g (10 oz) **macaroni** or
  orzo pasta
2 **eggs**
2 **egg yolks**
4 tablespoons chopped
  parsley, plus extra to garnish
  (optional)
salt and **pepper**
lemon rind curls, to garnish
  (optional)

Preheat the slow cooker if necessary; see the
manufacturer's instructions. Put the chicken, onion and
herbs into the slow cooker pot. Mix the stock, lemon rind
and juice and salt and pepper then pour over the chicken.

Cover with the lid and cook on high for 30 minutes.
Reduce the heat and cook on low for 5½–7½ hours, or
set to auto for 6–8 hours, until the chicken is cooked
through and tender. When almost ready to serve, bring
a large saucepan of water to the boil, add the pasta
and cook for 9–10 minutes or until just tender.

Meanwhile, drain the stock from the slow cooker pot
into a second large saucepan and boil for 5 minutes
until reduced by one-third or to about 200 ml (7 fl oz).
Whisk the eggs and egg yolks in a bowl, then gradually
whisk in 2 ladlefuls of stock until smooth. Pour into the
reduced stock, then whisk over a gentle heat until the
sauce has thickened slightly. Stir in the parsley.

Pour the sauce over the chicken. Spoon the pasta into
shallow bowls and top with the chicken. Sprinkle with
lemon rind curls and extra chopped parsley, if liked.

For salmon avgolemeno, lower a 500 g (1 lb) thick
piece of salmon into the slow cooker pot over a double
thickness strip of foil, add 6 thinly sliced spring onions
and the oregano or basil. Pour over 350 ml (12 fl oz)
boiling fish stock mixed with the lemon rind and juice
and salt and pepper. Cover and cook on low for 2½–3
hours or until the fish flakes easily when pressed in the
centre with a knife. Cook the pasta and make the sauce
as above. Lift the salmon out with the foil, skin and flake
into large chunks, then toss with the sauce and pasta.

vegetarian

mushroom & tomato rigatoni

Preparation time **20 minutes**
Cooking temperature **high**
Cooking time **2½–3 hours**
Serves **4**

250 g (8 oz) **rigatoni** or **pasta quills**
3 tablespoons **olive oil**
1 **onion**, sliced
2–3 **garlic cloves**, finely chopped
250 g (8 oz) **cup mushrooms**, sliced
250 g (8 oz) **portabella mushrooms**, sliced
250 g (8 oz) **tomatoes**, cut into chunks
400 g (13 oz) can **chopped tomatoes**
200 ml (7 fl oz) **vegetable stock** or **dry white wine**
1 tablespoon **tomato purée**
3 sprigs of **rosemary**
salt and **pepper**
freshly grated **Parmesan cheese**, to serve

Preheat the slow cooker if necessary; see the manufacturer's instructions. Put the pasta into a large bowl, cover with boiling water and leave to stand for 10 minutes while preparing the rest of the dish.

Heat 1 tablespoon of the oil in a large frying pan, add the onion and fry until softened. Stir in the remaining oil, garlic and mushrooms and fry, stirring, until the mushrooms are just beginning to brown.

Stir in the fresh and canned tomatoes, stock or wine and tomato purée. Add the rosemary and a little salt and pepper and bring to the boil.

Drain the pasta and put it in the slow cooker pot, pour over the hot mushroom mixture and spread into an even layer. Cover with the lid and cook on low for 2½–3 hours or until the pasta is just tender. Spoon into shallow bowls and sprinkle with grated Parmesan. Serve with a rocket salad.

For mushroom pastichio, replace the rigatoni or quills with 250 g (8 oz) macaroni and continue as above. Mix 3 eggs with 250 g (8 oz) natural yogurt, 75 g (3 oz) grated feta cheese and a pinch of grated nutmeg. Spoon over the top of the cooked mushroom and pasta mix for the last hour of cooking until set. Lift the pot out of the housing using oven gloves and brown under a hot grill.

goulash

1 tablespoon **sunflower oil**
1 **onion**, chopped
250 g (8 oz) **swede**, diced
250 g (8 oz) **carrots**, diced
250 g (8 oz) **potatoes**, diced
1 **red pepper**, cored,
  deseeded and diced
2 **celery sticks**, sliced
150 g (5 oz) **cup**
  mushrooms, halved
1 teaspoon **smoked paprika**,
  plus extra to garnish
  (optional)
¼ teaspoon **crushed dried**
  red chillies
1 teaspoon **caraway seeds**
1 tablespoon **plain flour**
400 g (13 oz) can **chopped**
  tomatoes
300 ml (½ pint) **vegetable**
  stock
2 **bay leaves**
salt and **pepper**
150 ml (¼ pint) **soured**
  cream, to serve

Preheat the slow cooker if necessary; see the
manufacturer's instructions. Heat the oil in a large
frying pan, add the onion and fry, stirring, until softened.
Add the vegetables, fry for 1–2 minutes, then stir in
the paprika, chillies and caraway seeds and cook for
1 minute.

Stir in the flour, then mix in the canned tomatoes and
stock, add the bay leaves and a little salt and pepper
and bring to the boil. Transfer to the slow cooker
pot and press the vegetables below the surface of
the liquid. Cover with the lid and cook on high for
4–5 hours or until the root vegetables are tender.

Stir the goulash and discard the bay leaves. Spoon
on to plates and top with spoonfuls of soured cream
and a sprinkling of extra paprika, if liked. Serve with
plain boiled rice.

For pork goulash, fry 750 g (1½ lb) diced lean
shoulder of pork in the oil until just beginning to
brown. Add the onion and fry until both are lightly
browned. Add the red pepper and 100 g (3½ oz)
sliced mushrooms, then stir in the paprika, chillies,
and caraway seeds, omitting the root vegetables
and celery. Continue as above, but cook on low for
8–10 hours.

beetroot & mascarpone risotto

Preparation time **20 minutes**
Cooking temperature **low**
Cooking time **1¾–2 hours**
Serves **4**

25 g (1 oz) **butter**
1 tablespoon **olive oil**
1 **red onion**, chopped
1 **garlic clove**, finely chopped
250 g (8 oz) pack **beetroot**
   in natural juice, drained
   and diced
250 g (8 oz) **risotto rice**
150 ml (¼ pint) **red wine**
1 litre (1¾ pints) **vegetable**
   stock
2 sprigs of **thyme**
salt and **pepper**

To serve
150 g (5 oz) **mascarpone**
   cheese
4 teaspoons chopped **thyme**
   leaves
Parmesan cheese shavings

Preheat the slow cooker if necessary; see the manufacturer's instructions. Heat the butter and oil in a large frying pan, add the onion and fry, stirring, for 5 minutes or until softened.

Stir in the garlic, beetroot and rice and cook for 1 minute, then mix in the wine and stock. Add the thyme and a little salt and pepper and bring to the boil, stirring.

Pour the mixture into the slow cooker pot. Cover with the lid and cook on low for 1¾–2 hours or until the rice is tender and almost all the stock has been absorbed.

Spoon into bowls and top with spoonfuls of mascarpone mixed with thyme, a little extra pepper and a generous sprinkling of Parmesan shavings.

For mushroom & thyme risotto, soak 15 g (½ oz) dried porcini mushrooms in 150 ml (¼ pint) boiling water for 15 minutes. Fry the onion in butter and oil as above, then add the garlic, 250 g (8 oz) mixed sliced mushrooms and an extra 25 g (1 oz) butter and fry briefly. Omit the beetroot. Add the rice and cook for 1 minute, then add the soaked mushrooms and their soaking liquid, the red wine, stock, thyme and salt and pepper and bring to the boil. Continue as above.

tomato & squash curry

Preparation time **20 minutes**
Cooking temperature **low**
Cooking time **5–6 hours**
Serves **4**

25 g (1 oz) **butter**
1 **onion**, chopped
½ **butternut squash**, about
    400 g (13 oz), peeled,
    deseeded and diced
2 **garlic cloves**, finely
    chopped
3.5 cm (1½ inch) **fresh root
    ginger**, peeled and finely
    chopped
½–1 mild **red chilli**, to taste,
    deseeded and finely
    chopped
4 tablespoons **korma curry
    paste**
150 ml (¼ pint) **vegetable
    stock**
8 **plum tomatoes**, about
    625 g (1¼ lb) in total, halved
50 g (2 oz) **creamed
    coconut**, crumbled
salt and **pepper**
roughly chopped **coriander**,
    to garnish

Preheat the slow cooker if necessary; see the manufacturer's instructions. Heat the butter in a large frying pan, add the onion and fry until softened.

Stir in the butternut squash, garlic, ginger and chilli and cook for 2–3 minutes. Mix in the curry paste and cook for 1 minute to release the curry flavour. Stir in the stock and bring to the boil.

Transfer the mixture to the slow cooker pot. Arrange the tomatoes, cut side uppermost, in a single layer on top of the squash, then sprinkle with the coconut and a little salt and pepper. Cover with the lid and cook on low for 5–6 hours or until the squash is tender and the tomatoes are soft but still holding their shape.

Spoon into bowls, sprinkle with roughly chopped coriander and serve with plain or pilau rice (see below) and naan bread.

For quick pilau rice to accompany the curry, rinse 225 g (7½ oz) basmati rice with cold water several times, then drain. Heat 15 g (½ oz) butter and 1 tablespoon sunflower oil in a large frying pan, add 1 chopped onion and fry until softened. Stir in 1 dried red chilli, 1 cinnamon stick, halved, 1 teaspoon cumin seeds, 1 bay leaf, 6 crushed cardamom pods, ½ teaspoon turmeric and some salt. Pour on 475 ml (16 fl oz) boiling water, cover with a lid and simmer gently for 10 minutes. Take off the heat and leave for 5–8 minutes – don't be tempted to lift the lid until ready to serve – then fluff up with a fork and spoon on to plates.

aubergines with baked eggs

Preparation time **20 minutes**
Cooking temperature **high**
Cooking time **2¾–3 hours**
  20 minutes
Serves **4**

4 tablespoons **olive oil**
1 **onion**, chopped
2 medium **aubergines**, cubed
2 **garlic cloves**, finely
  chopped
500 g (1 lb) **tomatoes**, cut
  into large chunks
½ teaspoon **smoked paprika**
½ teaspoon **ground cumin**
½ teaspoon **ground coriander**
100 g (3½ oz) **quinoa**
300 ml (½ pint) **vegetable
  stock**
125 g (4 oz) frozen **peas**
  (optional)
4 **eggs**
salt and **pepper**
chopped **mint**, to garnish

Preheat the slow cooker if necessary; see the manufacturer's instructions. Heat the oil in a large frying pan, add the onion and aubergines and fry, stirring, until the aubergines are golden.

Stir in the garlic, tomatoes and spices and cook for 1 minute. Mix in the quinoa and stock, add a little salt and pepper and bring to the boil. Transfer the mixture to the slow cooker pot. Cover with the lid and cook on high for 2½–3 hours.

Stir in the frozen peas, if using, and add a little boiling water if the quinoa has begun to stick around the edges of the pot. Make 4 dips with a spoon, then break and drop an egg into each dip. Cover and cook for 15–20 minutes or until the egg whites are set and the yolks still soft.

Spoon on to plates, sprinkle the eggs with a little extra salt and pepper and garnish with chopped mint. Serve with toasted pitta breads, cut into strips.

For aubergine ratatouille with baked eggs, omit the ground spices and quinoa and make up the recipe as above, adding 1 diced courgette and 1 cored, deseeded and diced orange pepper with the garlic, tomatoes and smoked paprika. Add 200 ml (7 fl oz) vegetable stock, season with salt and pepper and continue as above, omitting the peas. Serve sprinkled with torn basil leaves, spooned over toasted rustic-style bread.

pepperonata

Preparation time **20 minutes**
Cooking temperature **high**
Cooking time **3–4 hours**
Serves **3–4**

2 tablespoons **olive oil**
1 **onion**, chopped
3 **different coloured peppers**, cored, deseeded and diced
2 **garlic cloves**, finely chopped
1 tablespoon **plain flour**
400 g (13 oz) can **chopped tomatoes**
1 teaspoon **caster sugar**
2 sprigs of **basil**
150 ml (¼ pint) **vegetable stock**
500 g (1 lb) pack chilled **gnocchi**
salt and **pepper**
basil leaves, to garnish
freshly grated **Parmesan cheese**, to serve

Preheat the slow cooker if necessary; see the manufacturer's instructions. Heat the oil in a large frying pan, add the onion and fry, stirring until softened. Add the peppers and garlic and fry for 1–2 minutes.

Stir in the flour, mix in the tomatoes, then add the sugar, the basil, torn into pieces, stock and a little salt and pepper. Bring to the boil, then pour into the slow cooker pot. Cover with the lid and cook on high for 3–4 hours or until the peppers are tender.

When almost ready to serve, bring a large saucepan of water to the boil, add the gnocchi and cook for 2–3 minutes or until they float to the surface and are piping hot. Drain and gently stir into the pepperonata in the slow cooker pot. Spoon into shallow bowls and sprinkle with torn basil leaves and grated Parmesan.

For pepperonata & white bean stew, add a 410 g (13½ oz) can drained haricot beans to the stew when adding the tomatoes. Continue as above, omitting the gnocchi. Thickly slice and toast some ciabatta bread, rub the toast with a cut garlic clove and drizzle with a little olive oil. Serve with the stew.

spiced date & chickpea pilaf

Preparation time **15 minutes**
Cooking temperature **low**
Cooking time **3–4 hours**
Serves **4**

1 tablespoon **olive oil**
1 **onion**, chopped
1–2 **garlic cloves**, finely
    chopped
4 cm (1½ inches) **fresh root
    ginger**, peeled and finely
    chopped
1 teaspoon **turmeric**
1 teaspoon **ground cumin**,
    plus extra to garnish
1 teaspoon **ground coriander**
200 g (7 oz) easy-cook **brown
    rice**
410 g (13½ oz) can
    chickpeas, drained
75 g (3 oz) ready-chopped
    stoned **dates**
1 litre (1¾ pints) **vegetable
    stock**
salt and **pepper**

Onion garnish
1 tablespoon **olive oil**
1 **onion**, thinly sliced
150 g (5 oz) **Greek yogurt**
chopped **coriander**

Preheat the slow cooker if necessary; see the manufacturer's instructions. Heat the oil in a large frying pan, add the onion and fry, stirring, for 5 minutes or until softened and just beginning to turn golden.

Stir in the garlic, ginger and ground spices and cook for 1 minute. Add the rice, chickpeas, dates, stock and a little salt and pepper and bring to the boil, stirring. Pour into the slow cooker pot, cover with the lid and cook on low for 3–4 hours or until the rice is tender and almost all the stock has been absorbed.

Meanwhile, make the onion garnish. Heat the oil in a frying pan, add the sliced onion and fry over a medium heat, stirring, until crisp and golden. Stir the pilaf, spoon into bowls and top with a spoonful of yogurt, a little extra cumin, the onions and a little chopped coriander.

For chicken & almond pilaf, add 500 g (1 lb) diced boneless, skinless chicken thighs to the frying pan with the onion. Continue as above, omitting the dates. To serve, replace the onion garnish with 40 g (1½ oz) flaked almonds, fried in the oil until golden, and a little chopped mint, if liked.

barley risotto with blue cheese

Preparation time **20 minutes**
Cooking temperature **low**
Cooking time **6¼–8¼ hours**
Serves **4**

175 g (6 oz) **pearl barley**
1 **onion**, finely chopped
2 **garlic cloves**, finely
  chopped
500 g (1 lb) **butternut
  squash**, peeled, deseeded
  and cut into 2 cm (¾ inch)
  pieces
1 litre (1¾ pints) boiling
  vegetable stock
125 g (4 oz) baby **spinach**,
  washed and well drained

Blue cheese butter
100 g (3½ oz) **butter**, at room
  temperature
100 g (3½ oz) **blue cheese**
  (rind removed)
1 **garlic clove**, finely chopped
¼ teaspoon **crushed dried
  red chillies**
salt and **pepper**

Preheat the slow cooker if necessary; see the manufacturer's instructions. Put the pearl barley, onion, garlic and butternut squash into the slow cooker pot. Add the stock and a little salt and pepper. Cover with the lid and cook on low for 6–8 hours or until the barley and squash are tender.

Meanwhile, make the blue cheese butter. Put the butter on a plate, crumble the cheese on top, add the garlic and chillies and mash together with a fork. Spoon the butter into a line on a piece of nonstick baking paper, then wrap it in paper and roll it backwards and forwards to make a neat sausage shape. Chill in the refrigerator until required.

When almost ready to serve, stir the risotto, slice half the blue cheese butter and add to the slow cooker pot. Mix together until just beginning to melt, then add the spinach. Replace the lid and cook, still on low, for 15 minutes or until the spinach has just wilted. Ladle into shallow bowls and top with slices of the remaining butter.

For barley risotto with garlic & coriander cream, make up the risotto as above, replacing the squash with 500 g (1 lb) sweet potato and adding 150 g (5 oz) sliced cup mushrooms with the stock. Cook as above, omitting the spinach and blue cheese butter. Mix together 200 g (7 oz) crème fraîche, 1 finely chopped garlic clove, 3 tablespoons finely chopped coriander and 3 chopped spring onions. Ladle the risotto into bowls and top with spoonfuls of the cream.

cauliflower & spinach balti

Preparation time **10 minutes**
Cooking temperature **low**
Cooking time **5¼–6¼ hours**
Serves **4**

1 tablespoon **sunflower oil**
1 **onion**, chopped
540 g (1 lb 3 oz) can **balti curry sauce**
1 large **cauliflower**, trimmed and cut into large pieces, about 750 g (1½ lb) prepared weight
410 g (13½ oz) can **green lentils**, drained
150 g (5 oz) **spinach**, washed and torn into pieces

Preheat the slow cooker if necessary; see the manufacturer's instructions. Heat the oil in a large frying pan, add the onion and fry, stirring, for 5 minutes or until softened. Add the curry sauce and bring to the boil.

Put the cauliflower and lentils into the slow cooker pot, then pour over the hot sauce. Cover with the lid and cook on low for 5–6 hours or until the cauliflower is tender.

Stir the cauliflower and lentil mixture and sprinkle the spinach on top. Replace the lid and cook, still on low, for 10–15 minutes or until the spinach has just wilted. Spoon into bowls and serve with warm naan bread.

For mushroom & sweet potato balti, make up the sauce as above. Replace the cauliflower with 375 g (12 oz) quartered cup mushrooms and 375 g (12 oz) diced sweet potatoes and put into the slow cooker pot with the lentils. Pour over the sauce, cover with the lid and cook on low for 6–7 hours or until the sweet potatoes are tender. Add the spinach and cook and serve as above.

aubergine timbale

Preparation time **25 minutes**
Cooking temperature **high**
Cooking time **1½–2 hours**
Serves **2**

4 tablespoons **olive oil**, plus
   extra for greasing
1 large **aubergine**, thinly
   sliced
1 small **onion**, chopped
1 **garlic clove**, finely chopped
½ teaspoon **ground cinnamon**
¼ teaspoon grated **nutmeg**
25 g (1 oz) **pistachio nuts**,
   roughly chopped
25 g (1 oz) stoned **dates**,
   roughly chopped
25 g (1 oz) ready-to-eat dried
   apricots, roughly chopped
75 g (3 oz) easy-cook **long-
   grain rice**
300 ml (½ pint) boiling
   vegetable stock
salt and **pepper**

Preheat the slow cooker if necessary; see the
manufacturer's instructions. Lightly oil the base of
2 soufflé dishes, each 350 ml (12 fl oz), and base-line
each with a circle of nonstick baking paper, checking
first that they will fit in the slow cooker pot.

Heat 1 tablespoon of the oil in a large frying pan, add
one-third of the aubergines and fry on both sides until
softened and golden. Scoop out of the pan with a
slotted spoon and transfer to a plate. Repeat with the
rest of the aubergines using 2 more tablespoons of oil.

Heat the remaining 1 tablespoon of oil in the pan, add
the onion and fry for 5 minutes or until softened. Stir in
the garlic, spices, nuts, fruit and rice. Add a little salt
and pepper and mix well.

Arrange one-third of the aubergine slices in the base
of the 2 dishes, overlapping the slices. Spoon one-
quarter of the rice mixture into each dish, add a second
layer of aubergine slices, then divide the remaining rice
equally between the dishes. Top with the remaining
aubergine slices. Pour the stock into the dishes, cover
with lightly oiled foil and put in the slow cooker pot.

Pour boiling water into the pot to come halfway up the
sides of the dishes. Cover with the lid and cook on high
for 1½–2 hours or until the rice is tender. Lift the dishes
out of the slow cooker pot using a tea towel and
remove the foil. Loosen the edges of the timbales with
a knife, turn out on to plates and peel off the lining
paper. Serve hot with a green salad or baked tomatoes.

balsamic tomatoes with spaghetti

Preparation time **10 minutes**
Cooking temperature **high**
Cooking time **3–4 hours**
Serves **4**

1 tablespoon **olive oil**, for
    greasing
750 g (1½ lb) **plum tomatoes**,
    halved
4 tablespoons **white wine**
4 teaspoons good **balsamic
    vinegar**
375 g (12 oz) **spaghetti**
salt and **pepper**
basil leaves, to garnish
freshly grated or shaved
    Parmesan cheese, to serve

Preheat the slow cooker if necessary; see the manufacturer's instructions. Brush the oil over the base of the slow cooker pot, add the tomatoes, cut side down, drizzle over the wine and vinegar and add a little salt and pepper. Cover with the lid and cook on high for 3–4 hours or until the tomatoes are tender.

When almost ready to serve, bring a large saucepan of water to the boil, add the pasta and cook for 6–7 minutes or until tender. Drain and mix into the sauce. Spoon the pasta into bowls and sprinkle with basil leaves and grated or shaved Parmesan.

For pesto baked tomatoes, oil the base of the slow cooker pot as above, sprinkling with 2 finely chopped garlic cloves before adding the tomatoes. Drizzle with the wine and 1 tablespoon pesto sauce, omitting the vinegar. Cook and serve as above.

herby stuffed peppers

Preparation time **20 minutes**
Cooking temperature **low**
Cooking time **4–5 hours**
Serves **4**

4 **different coloured peppers**
100 g (3½ oz) easy-cook
  brown rice
410 g (13½ oz) can
  chickpeas, drained
small bunch of **parsley**,
  roughly chopped
small bunch of **mint**, roughly
  chopped
1 **onion**, finely chopped
2 **garlic cloves**, finely
  chopped
½ teaspoon **smoked paprika**
1 teaspoon **ground allspice**
600 ml (1 pint) boiling
  vegetable stock
salt and **pepper**

Preheat the slow cooker if necessary; see the
manufacturer's instructions. Cut the top off each
pepper, then remove the core and seeds.

Mix together the rice, chickpeas, herbs, onion, garlic,
paprika, allspice and plenty of salt and pepper in a bowl.
Spoon the mixture into the peppers, then put the
peppers into the slow cooker pot.

Pour the hot stock around the peppers, cover with the
lid and cook on low for 4–5 hours or until the rice and
peppers are tender. Spoon into dishes and serve with
salad and spoonfuls of Greek yogurt flavoured with
extra chopped herbs, if liked.

For chillied stuffed peppers, fry the onion in
1 tablespoon olive oil until softened. Stir in the garlic
and ½ teaspoon each of hot paprika or chilli powder,
ground allspice, ground cinnamon and ground cumin.
Mix with the brown rice and a drained 410 g (13½ oz)
can red kidney beans instead of the chickpeas.
Spoon into the peppers and put into the slow cooker.
Stir 2 tablespoons tomato puree into the stock and
continue as above.

tarka dhal

Preparation time **15 minutes**
Cooking temperature **high**
Cooking time **3–4 hours**
Serves **4**

250 g (8 oz) **red lentils**
1 **onion**, finely chopped
½ teaspoon **turmeric**
½ teaspoon **cumin seeds**,
  roughly crushed
2 cm (¾ inch) **fresh root
  ginger**, peeled and finely
  chopped
200 g (7 oz) canned **chopped
  tomatoes**
600 ml (1 pint) boiling
  vegetable stock
salt and **pepper**
coriander leaves, to garnish
150 g (5 oz) **natural yogurt**,
  to serve

Tarka

1 tablespoon **sunflower oil**
2 teaspoons **black mustard
  seeds**
½ teaspoon **cumin seeds**,
  roughly crushed
pinch of **turmeric**
2 **garlic cloves**, finely
  chopped

Preheat the slow cooker if necessary; see the
manufacturer's instructions. Rinse the lentils well with
cold water, drain and put into the slow cooker pot with
the onion, spices, ginger, tomatoes and boiling stock.
Stir in a little salt and pepper, cover with the lid and
cook on high for 3–4 hours or until the lentils are soft.

When almost ready to serve, make the tarka. Heat the
oil in a small frying pan, add the mustard and cumin
seeds, turmeric and garlic and fry, stirring, for 2 minutes.
Roughly mash the lentil mixture and spoon it into bowls.
Top with spoonfuls of yogurt and drizzle with the tarka.
Garnish with torn coriander leaves and serve with warm
naan bread.

For spinach & egg tarka dhal, cook the lentils as
above. Put 4 eggs in a pan of cold water, bring to the
boil and simmer for 8 minutes. Drain, peel and halve
the eggs. Twenty minutes before the end of the lentil
cooking time, add the eggs to the slow cooker pot
with 250 g (8 oz) finely shredded spinach and press
below the surface of the sauce. Replace the lid and
continue cooking. Serve with the tarka, yogurt and
coriander as above.

food for
friends

salmon-wrapped cod with leeks

Preparation time **30 minutes**
Cooking temperature **low**
Cooking time **1½–2 hours**
Serves **4**

2 **cod loins**, about 750 g
  (1½ lb) in total
juice of 1 **lemon**
4 sprigs of **dill**, plus extra to
  garnish (optional)
4 slices of **smoked salmon**,
  about 175 g (6 oz) in total
1 **leek**, thinly sliced; white and
  green parts kept separate
4 tablespoons **Noilly Prat**
200 ml (7 fl oz) boiling **fish
  stock**
2 teaspoons drained **capers**
  (optional)
75 g (3 oz) **butter**, diced
2 tablespoons chopped
  chives or **parsley**
salt and **pepper**

Preheat the slow cooker if necessary; see the manufacturer's instructions. Cut each cod loin in half to give 4 portions, then drizzle with the lemon juice and sprinkle with salt and pepper. Add a dill sprig to the top of each portion, then wrap with a slice of smoked salmon.

Put the white leek slices into the base of the slow cooker pot, arrange the fish on top in a single layer, tilting them slightly at an angle, if needed, to make them fit. Add the Noilly Prat and hot stock, then cover and cook on low for 1½–2 hours or until the fish flakes easily when pressed in the centre with a knife.

Lift out the fish with a fish slice and put it on a serving plate, cover with foil and keep hot. Pour the white leeks and cooking juices from the slow cooker pot into a saucepan, add the reserved green leek slices and the capers, if using, and boil rapidly for about 5 minutes or until the liquid is reduced to 4–6 tablespoons. Scoop out and reserve the leeks as soon as the green slices have softened.

Whisk in the butter, a piece at a time until melted, and continue until all the butter has been added and the sauce is smooth and glossy. Return the cooked leeks to the sauce with the chopped herbs and taste and adjust the seasoning. Arrange the fish on plates, then spoon the sauce around. Sprinkle with extra dill, if liked, and serve with baby new potatoes.

For smoked cod with buttered leeks, make up the recipe as above, with smoked cod loins, omitting the smoked salmon and dill and replacing the Noilly Prat with dry white wine.

venison puff pie

Preparation time **35 minutes**
Cooking temperature **low**
Cooking time **8–10 hours**
Serves **4–5**

25 g (1 oz) **butter**
1 tablespoon **olive oil**, plus
  extra for greasing
750 g (1½ lb) **venison**, diced
1 **onion**, chopped
2 tablespoons **plain flour**
200 ml (7 fl oz) **red wine**
250 ml (8 fl oz) **lamb** or **beef
  stock**
3 medium raw **beetroot**,
  peeled and cut into 1 cm
  (½ inch) dice
1 tablespoon **redcurrant jelly**
1 tablespoon **tomato purée**
10 **juniper berries**, roughly
  crushed
3 sprigs of **thyme**
1 **bay leaf**
1 sheet, about 200 g (7 oz),
  ready-rolled **puff pastry**
beaten **egg**, for glazing
salt and **pepper**

Preheat the slow cooker if necessary; see the manufacturer's instructions. Heat the butter and oil in a large frying pan, add the venison a few pieces at a time until all the pieces are in the pan, then fry, stirring, until evenly browned. Scoop the venison out of the pan with a slotted spoon and transfer to the slow cooker pot. Add the onion to the pan and fry for 5 minutes until softened.

Stir in the flour, then mix in the wine and stock. Add the beetroot, redcurrant jelly and tomato purée, then the juniper, 2 sprigs of thyme and the bay leaf. Season with salt and pepper and bring to the boil. Pour the sauce over the venison, cover with the lid and cook on low for 8–10 hours or until tender.

When you are almost ready to serve, preheat the oven to 220°C (425°F), Gas Mark 7. Unroll the pastry and trim the edges to make an oval similar in size to the slow cooker pot. Transfer to an oiled baking sheet, flute the edges and add leaves from the trimmings. Brush with egg, sprinkle with the remaining thyme leaves stripped from the stem and coarse salt and bake in the preheated oven for about 20 minutes until well risen and golden.

Stir the venison and spoon on to plates. Cut the pastry into wedges and place on top of the venison. Serve with roasted parsnips and baby carrots.

For lamb & mushroom puff pie, replace the venison with 750 g (1½ lb) diced shoulder or leg of lamb and fry as above. Fry the onion, then add 250 g (8 oz) quartered cup mushrooms in place of the beetroot and fry for 2–3 minutes. Stir in the flour and continue as above.

creamy chicken korma

Preparation time **15 minutes**
Cooking temperature **low**
Cooking time **6¼–7¼ hours**
Serves **4**

25 g (1 oz) **butter**

4 boneless, skinless **chicken breasts**, about 150 g (5 oz) each

1 **onion**, finely chopped

2 **garlic cloves**, finely chopped

2.5 cm (1 inch) **fresh root ginger**, peeled and finely chopped

3 tablespoons **korma curry paste**

4 tablespoons **ground almonds**

200 ml (7 fl oz) **chicken stock**

3 tablespoons **double cream**

3 tablespoons chopped **coriander**

salt and **pepper**

3 tablespoons toasted **flaked almonds**, to garnish

Preheat the slow cooker if necessary; see the manufacturer's instructions. Heat the butter in a large frying pan, add the chicken and fry on both sides until browned but not cooked through. Lift out of the pan with a slotted spoon and transfer to the slow cooker pot.

Add the onion, garlic and ginger to the pan and fry for 2–3 minutes, then stir in the curry paste and cook for 1 minute. Stir in the ground almonds, stock and salt and pepper and bring to the boil.

Pour the sauce over the chicken. Cover with the lid and cook on low for 6–7 hours or until the chicken is cooked through.

Stir in the cream and chopped coriander, replace the lid and cook, still on low, for 15 minutes. Slice the chicken. Spoon on to rice-lined plates and sprinkle with the almonds.

For creamy paneer korma, omit the chicken and fry 2 small very finely chopped onions in 25 g (1 oz) butter until softened. Add the garlic, ginger and curry paste, then stir in the ground almonds and stock and bring to the boil as above. Drain and cut 450 g (14½ oz) paneer (Indian cheese) into 2 cm (¾ inch) cubes and add to the slow cooker pot with the sauce. Continue as above.

braised duck with orange sauce

Preparation time **15 minutes**
Cooking temperature **high**
Cooking time **4–5 hours**
Serves **4**

4 **duck legs**, about 175 g
  (6 oz) each
1 **onion**, sliced
2 tablespoons **plain flour**
150 ml (¼ pint) **chicken stock**
150 ml (¼ pint) **dry white
  wine**
1 large **orange**, half sliced,
  half squeezed juice
1 **bay leaf**
1 teaspoon **Dijon mustard**
salt
½ teaspoon **black
  peppercorns**, roughly
  crushed

Preheat the slow cooker if necessary; see the
manufacturer's instructions. Dry-fry the duck in a large
frying pan over a low heat until the fat begins to run,
then increase the heat until the duck is browned on
both sides. Lift out of the pan with a slotted spoon and
transfer to the slow cooker pot.

Pour off any excess fat to leave about 1 tablespoon.
Fry the onions until softened. Stir in the flour, then mix
in the stock, wine, orange juice, bay leaf, a little salt and
the crushed peppercorns and bring to the boil, stirring.
Add the sliced orange.

Pour the sauce over the duck, cover with the lid and
cook on high for 4–5 hours or until the duck is tender
and almost falling off the bones. Serve with rice and
steamed green beans.

For braised duck with cranberries & port, fry the
duck and onions as above. Mix in the flour and stock,
then replace the wine with 150 ml (¼ pint) ruby port
and 100 g (3½ oz) fresh cranberries. Add orange
slices and juice and continue as above.

chillied beef with chocolate

Preparation time **15 minutes**
Cooking temperature **low**
Cooking time **8–10 hours**
Serves **4**

1 tablespoon **sunflower oil**
500 g (1 lb) **minced beef**
1 **onion**, chopped
3 **garlic cloves**, finely
   chopped
1 teaspoon **ground cinnamon**
1 teaspoon **ground cumin**
½–1 teaspoon **smoked or hot
   paprika**, plus extra to
   garnish
¼–½ teaspoon **crushed dried
   red chillies**
1 **bay leaf**
400 g (13 oz) can **chopped
   tomatoes**
410 g (13½ oz) can **red
   kidney beans**, drained
2 tablespoons **dark
   muscovado sugar**
300 ml (½ pint) **beef stock**
25 g (1 oz) **plain dark
   chocolate**
salt and **pepper**
soured cream, to serve

Preheat the slow cooker if necessary; see the manufacturer's instructions. Heat the oil in a frying pan, add the beef and onion and fry, stirring, until the mince is evenly browned.

Stir in the garlic, ground spices and bay leaf and cook for 1 minute. Mix in the tomatoes, beans, sugar and stock, then add the chocolate and a little salt and pepper and bring to the boil, stirring.

Pour into the slow cooker pot, cover with the lid and cook on low for 8–10 hours or until cooked through. Stir, spoon on to plates and top with a little soured cream, salsa (see below) and extra paprika. Serve with rice.

For avocado & red onion salsa to accompany the chillied beef, halve 1 large ripe avocado, remove the stone and peel away the skin. Dice the flesh, then toss in the grated rind and juice of 2 limes. Mix with 1 small finely chopped red onion, 1 chopped tomato and a small bunch of chopped coriander.

trout spirals with lemon foam

Preparation time **30 minutes**
Cooking temperature **low**
Cooking time **1½–2 hours**
Serves **4**

50 g (2 oz) **butter**, at room
  temperature
grated rind and juice of
  1 lemon
4 **trout fillets**, skinned, about
  650 g (1 lb 5 oz) in total
1 **plaice**, filleted into 4,
  skinned
200 ml (7 fl oz) boiling **fish
  stock**
3 **egg yolks**
salt and **pepper**

Preheat the slow cooker if necessary; see the manufacturer's instructions. Beat the butter with the lemon rind and a little salt and pepper.

Lay the trout fillets on a chopping board so that the skinned sides are uppermost. Trim the edges to neaten, if needed, and spread with half the lemon butter. Top with the plaice fillets, skinned side uppermost, and spread with the remaining butter. Roll up each fish stack, starting at the tapered end. Secure each spiral with 2 cocktail sticks at right angles to each other and arrange in the base of the slow cooker pot.

Pour the lemon juice and boiling stock over the fish and add a little salt and pepper. Cover with the lid and cook on low for 1½–2 hours or until the fish flakes easily when pressed in the centre with a knife.

Lift the fish spirals out of the slow cooker pot with a slotted spoon, put on to a serving plate and remove the cocktail sticks. Strain the cooking juices into a bowl. Put the egg yolks in a saucepan and gradually whisk in the strained stock until smooth. Cook over a medium heat, whisking constantly without boiling for 3–4 minutes or until lightly thickened and foamy. Pour into a jug. Serve the fish with a generous drizzle of the sauce around each one, salad and a separate bowl of tiny new potatoes.

For salmon steaks with lemon & tarragon foam, put 4 salmon steaks, about 150 g (5 oz) each and spread with the lemon butter, in the base of the slow cooker pot and continue as above. Make up the sauce as above, then whisk in 2 teaspoons chopped tarragon just before serving.

new orleans chicken gumbo

Preparation time **20 minutes**
Cooking temperature **low** and
high
Cooking time **8¼–10¼ hours**
Serves **4**

2 tablespoons **olive oil**
500 g (1 lb) boneless, skinless
chicken thighs, cubed
75 g (3 oz) ready-diced
chorizo
75 g (3 oz) **smoked streaky
bacon,** diced
1 **onion,** sliced
2 **garlic cloves,** chopped
2 tablespoons **plain flour**
600 ml (1 pint) **chicken stock**
2 **bay leaves**
2 sprigs of **thyme**
salt
¼–½ teaspoon **cayenne
pepper,** to taste
3 **celery sticks,** sliced
½ each of 3 different coloured
peppers, cored, deseeded
and sliced
125 g (4 oz) **okra,** thickly
sliced (optional)
chopped **parsley,** to garnish

Preheat the slow cooker if necessary; see the manufacturer's instructions. Heat the oil in a large frying pan, add the chicken a few pieces at time until all the pieces are in the pan, then add the chorizo and bacon and fry, stirring, until the chicken is golden. Lift out of the pan with a slotted spoon and transfer to the slow cooker.

Add the onion to the frying pan and fry until softened. Mix in the garlic, then stir in the flour. Gradually mix in the stock, add the herbs and a little salt and cayenne to taste. Bring to the boil, stirring.

Mix the celery and different coloured peppers into the chicken, then pour over the hot onion mixture. Cover with the lid and cook on low for 8–10 hours or until the chicken is cooked through.

When almost ready to serve, stir the okra into the chicken gumbo, if using. Replace the lid and cook on high for 15 minutes or until the okra has just softened. Stir once more, then sprinkle with chopped parsley. Ladle into shallow rice-lined bowls and serve with a soup spoon and fork.

For crab gumbo soup, omit the chicken and make up the gumbo as above, replacing the chicken stock with 600 ml (1 pint) fish stock and adding 2 sliced carrots, 2 diced sweet potatoes and 1 diced courgette to the slow cooker pot with the celery and peppers. Add 200 g (7 oz) large cooked king prawns, thawed if frozen, rinsed with cold water and drained, and a 200 g (7 oz) drained can white crab meat to the pot with the okra, if using, and cook on high for 20–30 minutes or until the fish is piping hot. Serve with rice.

tamarind beef with ginger beer

Preparation time **20 minutes**
Cooking temperature **low**
Cooking time **8–10 hours**
Serves **4**

2 tablespoons **sunflower oil**
750 g (1½ lb) lean **stewing beef**, cubed
1 **onion**, chopped
2 **garlic cloves**, finely chopped
2 tablespoons **plain flour**
330 ml can **ginger beer**
6 teaspoons **tamarind paste**
½ teaspoon **crushed dried red chillies**
1 teaspoon **ground mixed spice**
1 tablespoon **dark muscovado sugar**
salt and **pepper**

Preheat the slow cooker if necessary; see the manufacturer's instructions. Heat the oil in a large frying pan, add the beef a few pieces at a time until all the pieces are in the pan, then add the onion and fry over a medium heat, stirring, until the meat is evenly browned.

Stir in the garlic and flour. Gradually mix in the ginger beer, then stir in the tamarind paste, dried chillies and spice, sugar and a little salt and pepper and bring to the boil, stirring.

Transfer to the slow cooker pot and press the beef below the surface of the liquid. Cover with the lid and cook on low for 8–10 hours or until the meat is cooked through and tender.

Stir the beef, then ladle into bowls and top with garlic and coriander croutes (see below) and serve with steamed broccoli.

For ginger & coriander croutes to accompany the casserole, beat 2 cm (¾ inch) piece peeled and grated root ginger with 2 finely chopped garlic cloves and 50 g (2 oz) butter, stir in ½ mild, deseeded, finely chopped red chilli or a large pinch of dried crushed chillies, 3 tablespoons chopped coriander leaves and a little salt and pepper. Toast 8 slices of French bread on both sides and spread with the butter while hot. Arrange the croutes on top of the casserole and serve immediately.

fish pie

Preparation time **20 minutes**
Cooking temperature **low**
Cooking time **2–3 hours**
Serves **4–5**

1 tablespoon **sunflower oil**
1 **leek**, trimmed, cleaned and
  thinly sliced
50 g (2 oz) **butter**
50 g (2 oz) **plain flour**
450 ml (¾ pint) **UHT milk**
150 ml (¼ pint) **fish stock**
75 g (3 oz) **Cheddar cheese**,
  grated
1 **bay leaf**
800 g (1 lb 10 oz) mixed
  salmon, and **smoked** and
  unsmoked haddock,
  skinned and cut into large
  cubes
salt and **pepper**

Topping
4 tablespoons chopped
  parsley
800 g (1 lb 10 oz) hot
  homemade or bought
  mashed potato
25 g (1 oz) **butter**
15 g (½ oz) **Cheddar cheese**,
  grated

Preheat the slow cooker if necessary; see the manufacturer's instructions. Heat the oil in a saucepan, add the leek and fry, stirring, for 4–5 minutes or until softened. Scoop out of the pan with a slotted spoon and transfer to a plate.

Add the butter, flour and milk to the pan and bring to the boil, whisking constantly until thickened and smooth. Mix in the stock, cheese, bay leaf and a little salt and pepper.

Arrange the cubed fish in the slow cooker pot so that it is an even layer, then pour over the hot sauce. Cover with the lid and cook on low for 2–3 hours or until the fish flakes easily when pressed in the centre with a knife.

When almost ready to serve, stir the parsley into the hot mashed potatoes. Stir the fish, spoon into individual ovenproof dishes, if liked. Spoon the potatoes over the top, dot with the butter and sprinkle with the cheese. Lift the pot out of the housing using oven gloves if not using separate dishes and brown under the grill until golden. Serve with steamed asparagus.

For mixed fish & spinach gratin, wash 400 g (13 oz) baby spinach leaves in cold water, drain and place in a large saucepan. Cover and cook until just wilted. Transfer to a sieve and squeeze out as much water as possible. Spoon into the base of a 5 cm (2 inch) deep dish. Make up the fish pie mixture as above and spoon out of the slow cooker pot on to the spinach, then sprinkle with 50 g (2 oz) grated Cheddar and 4 tablespoons fresh breadcrumbs. Grill as above.

prune stuffed pork tenderloin

Preparation time **40 minutes**
Cooking temperature **high**
Cooking time **3½–4 hours**
Serves **4**

2 **pork tenderloins**, just under
 400 g (13 oz) each
1 slice of **bread**, crusts
 removed
1 small **onion**, quartered
2 **garlic cloves**, halved
4 cm (1½ inches) **fresh root
 ginger**, peeled and sliced
¼ teaspoon **ground allspice**
10 ready-to-eat stoned
 prunes
4 **smoked streaky bacon
 rashers**
1 tablespoon **olive oil**
12 **shallots**, halved if large
2 tablespoons **cornflour**
200 ml (7 fl oz) **red wine**
300 ml (½ pint) **chicken stock**
1 tablespoon **tomato purée**
salt and **pepper**

Preheat the slow cooker if necessary; see the
manufacturer's instructions. Trim the thinnest end off
each pork tenderloin so each is 23 cm (9 inches) long,
reserving the trimmings. Make a slit along the length of
each and open out flat.

Put the pork trimmings into a food processor with the
bread, onion, garlic, ginger, spice and salt and pepper
and mix until finely chopped. Spoon half the mixture
along the length of one piece of pork, press the prunes
on top, then cover with the rest of the stuffing and the
remaining tenderloin. Season, then wrap the bacon
around the pork and tie in place with string.

Heat the oil in a large frying pan, add the pork and
shallots and fry, turning the pork until golden all over.
Transfer to the slow cooker pot. Make a smooth paste
with the cornflour and a little cold water, then add to
the pan with the remaining ingredients. Bring to the
boil, stirring until thickened, then pour over the pork.

Cover with the lid and cook on high for 3½–4 hours or
until the pork is cooked through and tender. Transfer
the pork to a serving plate. Serve cut into thick slices,
with the shallots and sauce, accompanied with steamed
asparagus and creamy potato dauphinoise.

For apricot & pistachio stuffed pork tenderloin, slit
the tenderloins as above. Replace the prunes with
25 g (1 oz) roughly chopped pistachio nuts, grated rind
of ½ orange and 75 g (3 oz) chopped ready-to-eat dried
apricots and add to the pork trimmings mixture and
continue as above. To make the sauce, replace the red
wine with 200 ml (7 fl oz) dry cider.

beef & guinness puff pie

Preparation time **40 minutes**
Cooking temperature **low**
Cooking time **8–10 hours**
Serves **4–5**

2 tablespoons **sunflower oil**,
  plus extra for greasing
750 g (1½ lb) lean **stewing
  beef**, cubed
1 **onion**, chopped
2 tablespoons **plain flour**,
  plus extra for dusting
300 ml (½ pint) **Guinness**
150 ml (¼ pint) **beef stock**
2 teaspoons **hot horseradish**
1 tablespoon **tomato purée**
1 **bay leaf**
200 g (7 oz) **cup
  mushrooms**, sliced
salt and **pepper**

Pastry
500 g (1 lb) **puff pastry**,
  thawed if frozen
beaten **egg**, to glaze
100 g (3½ oz) **Stilton cheese**
  (rind removed), crumbled

Preheat the slow cooker if necessary; see the manufacturer's instructions. Heat the oil in a large frying pan, add the meat a few pieces at a time until all the pieces are in the pan, then add the onion and fry over a medium heat, stirring until the meat is evenly browned.

Stir in the flour, then gradually mix in the Guinness and the stock. Stir in the horseradish, tomato purée and a little salt and pepper, then add the bay leaf and bring to the boil. Transfer to the slow cooker pot and press the meat below the surface of the liquid. Cover with the lid and cook on low for 8–10 hours or until the meat is cooked through and very tender.

When almost ready to serve, preheat the oven to 200°C (400°F), Gas Mark 6. Discard the bay leaf and divide the beef mixture between 4 pie dishes, each about 450 ml (¾ pint). Mix in the mushrooms, then brush the top edge of the dishes with a little egg. Cut the pastry into 4 and roll each piece out on a floured surface until a little larger than the dishes, then press on to the dishes. Trim off the excess pastry and crimp the edges. Mark diagonal lines on top and brush with beaten egg. Put on an oiled baking sheet and cook in the preheated oven for 30 minutes or until golden. Sprinkle with the Stilton and leave to melt for 1–2 minutes. Serve with green beans and curly kale.

For beery beef hotpot, make up the meat base as above, omitting the mushrooms and adding 2 diced carrots. Spoon into the slow cooker pot, then cover with 700 g (1 lb 6 oz) thinly sliced potatoes, pressing them just below the stock. Cook as above. Dot 25 g (1 oz) butter over the potatoes, lift the pot out of the housing using oven gloves and brown under a hot grill.

slow-cooked lamb shanks

Preparation time **20 minutes**
Cooking temperature **high**
Cooking time **5–7 hours**
Serves **4**

2 tablespoons **olive oil**
4 **lamb shanks**, about 375 g
  (12 oz) each
625 g (1¼ lb) **new potatoes**,
  thickly sliced
2 **onions**, sliced
3–4 **garlic cloves**, finely
  chopped
300 ml (½ pint) **white wine**
150 ml (¼ pint) **lamb stock**
1 tablespoon **runny honey**
1 teaspoon **dried oregano**
75 g (3 oz) **preserved
  lemons**, cut into chunks
75 g (3 oz) **green olives**
  (optional)
salt and **pepper**
chopped **parsley**, to garnish

Preheat the slow cooker if necessary; see the manufacturer's instructions. Heat the oil in a large frying pan, add the lamb and fry, turning until browned on all sides. Arrange the potatoes in the base of the slow cooker pot, then put the lamb on top.

Add the onion to the pan and fry until softened, then mix in the garlic. Add the wine, stock, honey, oregano and a little salt and pepper and bring to the boil. Pour over the lamb, then add the lemons and olives, if using.

Cover with the lid and cook on high for 5–7 hours or until the potatoes are tender and the lamb is almost falling off the bone. Spoon into shallow bowls and sprinkle with parsley. Serve with a green salad.

For slow-cooked lamb shanks with prunes, fry the lamb as above and add to the potatoes. Fry the onion and garlic with 3 diced streaky bacon rashers, then mix in 300 ml (½ pint) red wine, 150 ml (¼ pint) lamb stock, 1 tablespoon tomato purée, 75 g (3 oz) pitted prunes, a small bunch of mixed herbs and salt and pepper. Cover and cook as above.

salmon & asparagus risotto

Preparation time **15 minutes**
Cooking temperature **low**
Cooking time **1¾–2 hours**
Serves **4**

25 g (1 oz) **butter**
1 tablespoon **olive oil**
1 **onion**, chopped
grated rind of 1 **lemon**
200 g (7 oz) **risotto rice**
150 ml (¼ pint) **dry white wine**
900 ml (1½ pints) **fish** or **vegetable stock**
4 **salmon steaks**, about 150 g (5 oz) each
1 bunch of **asparagus**, trimmed and thickly sliced
salt and **pepper**
125 ml (4 fl oz) **crème fraîche**, to serve
chopped **chives**, to garnish

Preheat the slow cooker if necessary; see the manufacturer's instructions. Heat the butter and oil in a large frying pan, add the onion and fry for 5 minutes or until softened. Stir in the lemon rind and rice and cook for 1 minute. Mix in the wine, stock and a little salt and pepper and bring to the boil, stirring.

Pour into the slow cooker pot. Arrange the salmon steaks in a single layer on the rice, turning on their sides, if needed, so they are just below the surface of the stock. Cover with the lid and cook on low for 1¾–2 hours or until the rice is tender and the salmon flakes into opaque pieces when pressed in the centre with a knife.

When almost ready to serve, bring a saucepan of water to the boil, add the asparagus and cook for 5 minutes or until just tender. Spoon the rice into shallow bowls and top with spoonfuls of crème fraîche, the drained asparagus and salmon steaks broken into pieces. Sprinkle with chopped chives and a little extra pepper.

For smoked fish kedgeree, add ½ teaspoon turmeric and 1 bay leaf to the fried onion instead of the lemon rind. Add 1 litre (1¾ pints) of stock, bring to the boil, then transfer to the slow cooker pot. Replace the salmon with 625 g (1¼ lb) smoked haddock, cut into 2 pieces, then cook as above. Skin and flake the fish, discard the bay leaf, then return to the pot and stir in 4 tablespoons double cream and 75 g (3 oz) just cooked frozen peas. Spoon into bowls and top with 4 hardboiled eggs cut into wedges. Sprinkle with chopped chives and a little extra black pepper.

puddings

mini banana & date puddings

Preparation time **20 minutes**
Cooking temperature **high**
Cooking time **2–3 hours**
Serves **4**

100 g (3½ oz) **butter**, at room
    temperature, plus extra for
    greasing
100 g (3½ oz) **light
    muscovado sugar**
2 **eggs**, beaten
125 g (4 oz) **self-raising flour**
1 small ripe **banana**, mashed
75 g (3 oz) ready-chopped
    stoned **dates**
250 g (8 oz) **ready-made
    toffee sauce**
50 g (2 oz) **plain dark
    chocolate**, broken into
    pieces

Preheat the slow cooker if necessary; see the manufacturer's instructions. Butter 4 metal pudding moulds, each 250 ml (8 fl oz), and base-line each with a circle of nonstick baking paper, checking first that they will fit in the slow cooker pot.

Beat the butter and sugar in a bowl with a wooden spoon or hand-held electric whisk until soft and creamy. Gradually add alternate spoonfuls of egg and flour until both have all been added and the mixture is smooth. Mash the banana on a plate, then beat into the pudding mix. Stir in the dates, then divide between the moulds.

Cover each one with a square of foil and stand in the slow cooker pot. Pour boiling water into the pot to come halfway up the sides of the moulds. Cover with the lid and cook on high for 2–3 hours or until the tops of the puddings spring back when pressed with a fingertip.

Lift the moulds from the slow cooker pot using a tea towel and remove the foil. Loosen the edges with a knife and turn out on to plates. Pour the toffee sauce into a small saucepan, add the chocolate and warm through, stirring until the chocolate has just melted. Drizzle over the puddings and serve immediately.

For mini chocolate & banana puddings, make up the puddings with the butter, sugar and eggs as above. Substitute 15 g (½ oz) cocoa for the same weight of flour, then add with the remaining flour, mashed banana and dates. Cook as above. Warm 4 tablespoons chocolate and hazelnut spread with 2 tablespoons double cream and 2 tablespoons milk in a saucepan, stir until smooth and serve with the puddings.

cider poached apples with granola

Preparation time **10 minutes**
Cooking temperature **high**
Cooking time **1½–2 hours**
Serves **4**

4 medium **cooking apples**,
  about 750 g (1½ lb) in total,
  peeled, cored and quartered
grated rind and juice of
  1 **lemon**
50 g (2 oz) **sultanas**
4 tablespoons **light**
  muscovado sugar
250 ml (8 fl oz) **dry cider**
15 g (½ oz) **butter**
125 g (4 oz) **crème fraîche**,
  to serve
ground cinnamon, to
  decorate

Almond granola
25 g (1 oz) **butter**
125 g (4 oz) **granola-style**
  cereal
2 tablespoons **flaked**
  almonds
2 tablespoons **light**
  muscovado sugar

Preheat the slow cooker if necessary; see the
manufacturer's instructions. Cut each apple quarter in
half again, then put into the slow cooker and toss with
the lemon rind and juice. Arrange the apples so that
they are in a single layer.

Sprinkle with the sultanas and sugar, pour over the
cider and dot with the butter. Cover with the lid and
cook on high for 1½–2 hours or until the apples are
tender but still holding their shape.

When almost ready to serve, heat the butter for the
almond granola in a frying pan, add the remaining
ingredients and fry, stirring until hot and browned.
Spoon the apples and the cidery juices into bowls
and sprinkle hot granola on top. Serve with cream or
ice cream.

For spiced poached apples with orange, arrange
the apples in the slow cooker pot as above, adding
the rind of 1 orange with the lemon juice and rind.
Replace the sultanas with 1 orange, peeled and cut
into segments, 1 cinnamon stick, broken into pieces,
and 4 cloves and sprinkle over the apples with the
sugar. Pour over 125 ml (4 fl oz) apple juice and
125 ml (4 fl oz) water instead of the cider and dot
with butter. Continue as above. Serve with scoops of
vanilla ice cream.

jam roly-poly pudding

Preparation time **25 minutes**
Cooking temperature **high**
Cooking time **3½–4 hours**
Serves **4**

300 g (10 oz) **self-raising flour**
150 g (5 oz) **vegetable suet**
50 g (2 oz) **caster sugar**
grated rind of 2 **lemons**
200–250 ml (7–8 fl oz) **milk** or **milk** and **water** mixed
4 tablespoons **strawberry jam**
salt

Preheat the slow cooker if necessary; see the manufacturer's instructions. Put the flour, suet, sugar, lemon rind and a pinch of salt in a bowl and mix well. Gradually stir in the milk or milk and water to make a soft but not sticky dough. Knead lightly, then roll out on a piece of floured nonstick baking paper to a rectangle about 23 x 30 cm (9 x 12 inches). Turn the paper so that the shorter edges are facing you.

Spread the jam over the pastry, leaving 2 cm (¾ inch) around the edges. Roll up, starting at a shorter edge, using the paper to help. Wrap in the paper, then in a sheet of foil. Twist the ends together tightly, leaving space for the pudding to rise.

Transfer the pudding to the slow cooker pot and raise off the base by standing it on 2 ramekin dishes. Pour boiling water into the pot to come a little up the sides of the pudding, being careful that the water cannot seep through any joins. Cover with the lid and cook on high for 3½–4 hours or until the pudding is light and fluffy. Lift out of the pot, then unwrap and cut into thick slices. Serve with hot custard.

For spotted dick, grate the rind of 1 large orange and reserve, squeeze the juice into a saucepan, bring to the boil, add 150 g (5 oz) raisins and leave to soak for 30 minutes. Make up the pastry as above, adding the orange rind, the grated rind of 1 lemon and the soaked raisins before mixing with enough milk to make a soft dough. Shape into a log 23 cm (9 inches) long. Wrap in nonstick baking paper and foil, then cook as above.

chocolate & coffee custard creams

Preparation time **20 minutes**, plus chilling
Cooking temperature **low**
Cooking time **3–3½ hours**
Serves **4**

450 ml (¾ pint) **milk**
100 g (3½ oz) **plain dark chocolate**, broken into pieces
1 teaspoon **instant coffee**
2 **eggs**
2 **egg yolks**
3 tablespoons **light muscovado sugar**
½ teaspoon **vanilla extract**
sifted **cocoa powder**, to decorate

Topping
125 ml (4 fl oz) **double cream**
2 tablespoons **light muscovado sugar**
½ teaspoon **vanilla extract**

Preheat the slow cooker if necessary; see the manufacturer's instructions. Pour the milk into a saucepan and bring just to the boil. Remove from the heat, add the chocolate pieces and instant coffee and set aside for 5 minutes, stirring occasionally, until the chocolate has melted.

Put the whole eggs, egg yolks, sugar and vanilla extract in a bowl and whisk until just mixed. Gradually whisk in the hot chocolate milk until smooth. Strain through a sieve into the pan, then pour into 4 tall heatproof mugs, each 250 ml (8 fl oz), checking first that they will fit in the slow cooker pot.

Cover the tops of the mugs with foil and stand them in the slow cooker pot. Pour boiling water into the pot to come halfway up the sides of the mugs. Cover with the lid and cook on low for 3–3½ hours or until the custards are set and the tops can be lightly pressed with a fingertip.

Lift the mugs carefully out of the slow cooker pot using a tea towel. Leave to cool, then transfer to the refrigerator for at least 4 hours until chilled. Just before serving, whip the cream with the sugar and vanilla until soft swirls form. Spoon the topping over the custards and lightly dust with cocoa powder. Serve with dainty biscuits.

For vanilla custard pots, bring the milk just to the boil as above. Whisk the whole eggs and egg yolks with 2 tablespoons caster sugar and 1 teaspoon vanilla extract. Gradually whisk in the hot milk, then strain and continue as above, sprinkling the tops with a little grated nutmeg before cooking, if liked.

184

topsy turvy plum pudding

Preparation time **25 minutes**
Cooking temperature **high**
Cooking time **4–5 hours**
Serves **6**

100 g (3½ oz) **butter**, at room
  temperature, plus extra for
  greasing
100 g (3½ oz) **blackberries**,
  thawed if frozen
200 g (7 oz) ripe **red plums**,
  halved, stoned and sliced
2 tablespoons **red berry jam**
100 g (3½ oz) **caster sugar**
100 g (3½ oz) **self-raising
  flour**
2 **eggs**, beaten
50 g (2 oz) **ground almonds**
few drops of **almond extract**
toasted **flaked almonds**, to
  decorate (optional)

Preheat the slow cooker if necessary; see the manufacturer's instructions. Lightly butter a 1.2 litre (2 pint) soufflé dish and base-line with a circle of nonstick baking paper, checking first that the dish will fit in the slow cooker pot. Arrange the blackberries and plums in the base, then dot with the jam.

Beat the butter and sugar in a bowl with a wooden spoon or hand-held electric whisk until soft and creamy. Gradually mix in alternate spoonfuls of flour and beaten egg, and continue adding and beating until the mixture is smooth. Stir in the almonds and almond extract. Spoon the mixture over the fruit, spread it level and cover the top with foil.

Lower the dish into the slow cooker pot and pour boiling water into the pot to come halfway up the sides of the dish. Cover with the lid and cook on high for 4–5 hours or until the sponge is well risen and springs back when pressed with a fingertip.

Lift the dish out of the slow cooker pot using a tea towel and remove the foil. Loosen the edges of the pudding with a knife and turn out on to a plate with a rim. Decorate with toasted flaked almonds, if liked, and serve hot with custard.

For peach & chocolate pudding, arrange 2 (or 1 if very large) halved, stoned and sliced ripe peaches in the base of the dish and dot with 2 tablespoons apricot jam. Make up the sponge mixture as above, adding 25 g (1 oz) cocoa powder and an extra 25 g (1 oz) self-raising flour instead of the ground almonds and almond extract. Continue as above.

hot chocolate mousses

Preparation time **25 minutes**
Cooking temperature **high**
Cooking time **1–1¼ hours**
Serves **4**

200 g (7 oz) **plain dark
  chocolate**, broken into
  pieces
50 g (2 oz) **butter**, plus extra
  for greasing
4 **eggs**, separated
4 tablespoons **caster sugar**
1 tablespoons **warm water**
sifted **icing sugar**, to decorate

Mint cream
6 tablespoons **double cream**
4 teaspoons chopped **mint**

Preheat the slow cooker if necessary; see the manufacturer's instructions. Put the chocolate and butter in a bowl, set over a saucepan of very gently simmering water making sure that the water does not touch the base of the bowl and leave until just melted.

Meanwhile, butter 4 mugs, each 250 ml (8 fl oz), checking first that they will fit in the slow cooker pot.

Whisk the egg whites in a bowl until soft peaks, then gradually whisk in the sugar a teaspoonful at a time until it has all been added and the meringue is thick and glossy. Take the bowl of chocolate off the saucepan, stir in the egg yolks and warm water and gently fold in a spoonful of the egg whites to loosen the mixture. Fold in the remaining egg whites, then divide between the mugs.

Cover the tops with domed foil and put into the slow cooker pot. Pour boiling water into the pot to come halfway up the sides of the mugs. Cover with the lid and cook on high for 1–1¼ hours or until the puddings are softly set in the centre.

Lift the puddings out of the slow cooker pot and remove the foil. Mix the cream and mint together and pour into a jug. Dust the puddings with icing sugar and serve immediately with the mint cream.

For gingered mousses with orange cream, add 4 teaspoons finely chopped stem ginger to the mousse mixture and cook as above. To serve, stir an extra 2 teaspoons finely chopped stem ginger and the finely grated rind of 1 orange into 6 tablespoons crème fraîche in a bowl.

apricot & orange fool

Preparation time **20 minutes**, plus cooling
Cooking temperature **low**
Cooking time **3–4 hours**
Serves **6**

250 g (8 oz) ready-to-eat dried **apricots**
grated rind and juice of 1 **orange**
2 tablespoons **caster sugar**
300 ml (½ pint) cold **water**
2 x 135 g (4½ oz) pots **ready-made custard**
500 g (1 lb) **natural yogurt**

Preheat the slow cooker if necessary; see the manufacturer's instructions. Put the apricots, orange rind and juice and sugar into the slow cooker pot and pour over the water. Cover with the lid and cook on low for 3–4 hours or until the apricots are plump.

Lift the pot out of the housing using oven gloves and leave the apricots to cool, then purée with a stick blender or transfer to a liquidizer and whizz until smooth.

Fold the custard and yogurt together until just mixed, then add the apricot purée and very lightly mix for a marbled effect. Spoon into the glasses and serve with dainty biscuits.

For prune & vanilla fool, put 250 g (8 oz) ready-to-eat stoned prunes, 1 teaspoon vanilla extract, 2 tablespoons honey and 300 ml (½ pint) cold water in the slow cooker pot and cook, cool and make up the fool as above.

berry compote with syllabub cream

Preparation time **20 minutes**,
  plus cooling
Cooking temperature **low**
Cooking time **1½–2 hours**
Serves **4**

500 g (1 lb) **strawberries**,
  halved or quartered if large
200 g (7 oz) **blueberries**
grated rind and juice of
  1 **lemon**
3 tablespoons **caster sugar**
3 tablespoons **water**

Syllabub cream
150 ml (¼ pint) **double cream**
2 tablespoons **caster sugar**
grated rind of ½ **lemon**
2 tablespoons **dry white wine**
lemon rind curls or small
  herb or **pansy flowers**, to
  decorate (optional)

Preheat the slow cooker if necessary; see the manufacturer's instructions. Put the fruit, lemon rind and juice, sugar and water into the slow cooker pot. Cover with the lid and cook on low for 1½–2 hours or until the fruit is tender but still holds its shape.

Lift the pot out of the housing using oven gloves and leave the compote to cool. Just before serving, make the syllabub. Pour the cream into a bowl, add the sugar and lemon rind and whisk until it forms soft swirls. Add the white wine and whisk for a further 1–2 minutes or until thick again.

Spoon the fruit into tall champagne-style glasses and top with spoonfuls of the cream. Decorate with small herb or pansy flowers, if liked, and serve immediately.

For peach compote with vanilla, halve 6 firm, ripe peaches and add to the slow cooker pot with 75 g (3 oz) caster sugar, 150 ml (¼ pint) Marsala or sweet sherry, 150 ml (¼ pint) water and a slit vanilla pod. Cover and cook as above. Transfer the peaches to a serving dish. Scrape the seeds from the vanilla pod and add to the syrup, then discard the pod. Mix 2 teaspoons cornflour with a little cold water to make a smooth paste, stir into the syrup in the slow cooker pot, replace the lid and cook on high for 15 minutes. Stir well, then pour over the peaches. Sprinkle with 125 g (4 oz) raspberries and leave to cool. Serve with spoonfuls of crème fraîche.

sticky marmalade syrup pudding

Preparation time **20 minutes**
Cooking temperature **high**
Cooking time **3–3½ hours**
Serves **4–5**

butter, for greasing
4 tablespoons **golden syrup**
3 tablespoons **orange marmalade**
175 g (6 oz) **self-raising flour**
75 g (3 oz) **vegetable suet**
50 g (2 oz) **light muscovado sugar**
1 teaspoon **ground ginger**
grated rind and juice of
1 **orange**
2 **eggs**
2 tablespoons **milk**

Preheat the slow cooker if necessary; see the manufacturer's instructions. Lightly butter a 1.2 litre (2 pint) pudding basin and base-line with a circle of nonstick baking paper, checking first that it will fit in the slow cooker pot. Spoon the golden syrup and 2 tablespoons of the marmalade into the basin.

Put the flour, suet, sugar and ginger in a bowl and mix together. Add the remaining marmalade, orange rind and juice, the eggs and milk and beat until smooth. Spoon the mixture into the basin, spread it level and cover the top with buttered foil.

Lower the basin into the slow cooker pot and pour boiling water into the pot to come halfway up the sides of the basin. Cover with the lid and cook on high for 3–3½ hours or until the pudding is well risen and feels firm and dry when the top is pressed with a fingertip.

Lift the basin out of the slow cooker pot using a tea towel and remove the foil. Loosen the edge of the pudding with a knife, turn out on to a plate and peel off the lining paper. Serve scoops of the pudding in bowls with custard or vanilla ice cream.

For sticky banana pudding, spoon 4 tablespoons golden syrup and 3 tablespoons light muscovado sugar into the base of the lined basin. Cut 2 bananas in half lengthways, then in half again crossways. Toss in the juice of ½ lemon and arrange cut side down in the bottom of the basin. Make up the pudding mixture, spoon over the bananas and continue as above.

194

strawberry cheesecake

Preparation time **30 minutes**,
 plus chilling
Cooking temperature **high**
Cooking time **2–2½ hours**
Serves **4–5**

4 **trifle sponges**
300 g (10 oz) **full-fat cream
 cheese**
75 g (3 oz) **caster sugar**
150 ml (¼ pint) **double cream**
3 **eggs**
grated rind and juice of
 ½ **lemon**

Topping
2 tablespoons **strawberry jam**
1 tablespoon **lemon juice**
200 g (7 oz) **strawberries**,
 hulled and sliced

Preheat the slow cooker if necessary; see the manufacturer's instructions. Line the base and sides of a soufflé dish, 14 cm (5½ inches) in diameter and 9 cm (3½ inches) high, with nonstick baking paper, checking first it will fit in the slow cooker pot. Line the base with the trifle sponges, trimming them to fit in a single layer.

Put the cream cheese and sugar in a bowl, then gradually whisk in the cream until smooth and thick. Gradually whisk in the eggs one at a time, then mix in the lemon rind and juice. Pour the mixture into the dish and spread it level.

Cover the top with buttered foil and lower it into the slow cooker pot. Pour boiling water into the pot to come halfway up the sides of the dish. Cover with the lid and cook on high for 2–2½ hours or until the cheesecake is well risen and softly set in the centre.

Lift the dish out of the slow cooker pot using a tea towel and leave to cool and firm up. The cheesecake will sink quickly as it cools to about the size that it was before cooking. Transfer to the refrigerator to chill for at least 4 hours.

When ready to serve, loosen the edge of the cheesecake with a knife, turn out on to a serving plate, peel off the lining paper and turn it the right way up. Mix the jam and lemon juice in a bowl until smooth, add the sliced strawberries and toss together. Spoon on top of the cheesecake and serve immediately.

hot toddy oranges

Preparation time **15 minutes**
Cooking temperature **low**
Cooking time **2–3 hours**
Serves **4**

8 **clementines**
50 g (2 oz) **honey**
75 g (3 oz) **light muscovado
    sugar**
grated rind and juice of
    ½ lemon
4 tablespoons **whisky**
300 ml (½ pint) boiling **water**
15 g (½ oz) **butter**

Preheat the slow cooker if necessary; see the manufacturer's instructions. Peel the clementines, leaving them whole. Put the remaining ingredients in the slow cooker pot and mix together.

Add the clementines. Cover with the lid and cook on low for 2–3 hours or until piping hot. Spoon into shallow bowls and serve with just-melting scoops of vanilla ice cream.

For hot toddy apricots, put all the ingredients, omitting the clementines and sugar, into the slow cooker pot as above. Add 300 g (10 oz) ready-to-eat dried apricots and continue as above. Serve warm with crème fraîche or vanilla ice cream.

peppermint & raspberry brûlée

Preparation time **30 minutes**, plus chilling
Cooking temperature **low**
Cooking time **2½–3½ hours**
Serves **4**

4 **egg yolks**
40 g (1½ oz) **caster sugar**
400 ml (14 fl oz) **double cream**
¼ teaspoon **peppermint extract**
150 g (5 oz) **raspberries**
2 tablespoons **icing sugar**

Preheat the slow cooker if necessary; see the manufacturer's instructions. Whisk the egg yolks and sugar in a bowl for 3–4 minutes until frothy, then gradually whisk in the cream. Stir in the peppermint extract, then strain the egg custard into a jug.

Pour into 4 ramekin dishes, each 150 ml (¼ pint), checking first that they will fit in the slow cooker pot. Put the dishes into the slow cooker pot, pour boiling water into the pot to come halfway up the sides of the dishes, then loosely cover the top of each dish with foil.

Cover with the lid and cook on low for 2½–3½ hours or until the custard is set with a slight quiver to the middle. Lift the dishes carefully out of the slow cooker and leave to cool. Transfer to the refrigerator to chill for 4 hours.

When ready to serve, pile a few raspberries in the centre of each dish and sprinkle over some icing sugar. Caramelize the sugar with a cook's blow torch.

For peppermint & white chocolate brûlée, bring 350 ml (12 fl oz) double cream just to the boil in a saucepan, take off the heat and add 100 g (4 oz) good-quality white chocolate, broken into pieces, and leave until melted. Whisk the egg yolks with 25 g (1 oz) caster sugar, then gradually mix in the chocolate cream and the peppermint extract. Continue as above. Replace the raspberries with blueberries and serve as above.

honeyed rice pudding

Preparation time **10 minutes**
Cooking temperature **low**
Cooking time **2½–3 hours**
Serves **4**

butter, for greasing
750 ml (1¼ pints) **full-fat Jersey milk**
3 tablespoons **set honey**
125 g (4 oz) **risotto rice**

Preheat the slow cooker if necessary; see the manufacturer's instructions. Lightly butter the inside of the slow cooker pot. Pour the milk into a saucepan, add the honey and bring just to the boil, stirring until the honey has melted. Pour into the slow cooker pot, add the rice and stir gently.

Cover with the lid and cook on low for 2½–3 hours, stirring once during cooking, or until the pudding is thickened and the rice is soft. Stir again just before spooning into dishes and serve topped with spoonfuls of jam, or the Apricot Conserve on page 222, and thick cream, if liked.

For vanilla rice pudding, pour the milk into a saucepan, replace the honey with 3 tablespoons caster sugar and bring just to the boil. Slit a vanilla pod, scrape the black seeds out with a small knife and add to the milk with the pod. Pour into the greased slow cooker pot, add the rice and cook as above. Remove the vanilla pod before serving with thick cream.

toffee apple pancakes

Preparation time **10 minutes**
Cooking temperature **high**
Cooking time **1–1½ hours**
Serves **4–6**

50 g (2 oz) **butter**
75 g (3 oz) **light muscovado sugar**
2 tablespoons **golden syrup**
4 **dessert apples,** cored and each cut into 8 slices
juice of 1 **lemon**
375 g (12 oz) pack or 6 **ready-made pancakes**
vanilla ice cream, to serve

Preheat the slow cooker if necessary; see the manufacturer's instructions. Heat the butter, sugar and syrup in a saucepan or in a bowl in the microwave until the butter has just melted.

Add the apples and lemon juice to the slow cooker pot and toss together. Stir the butter mix and pour it over the apples. Cover with the lid and cook on high for 1–1½ hours or until the apples are tender but still holding their shape.

Heat the pancakes in a frying pan or the microwave, according to the pack instructions. Fold in half and arrange on serving plates. Stir the apple mix, then spoon it on to the pancakes. Top with a scoop of vanilla ice cream.

For toffee banana pancakes, make up the recipe as above, replacing the apples with 6 small thickly sliced bananas and adding 150 ml (¼ pint) boiling water. When ready to serve, reheat 6 pancakes, spread with 3 tablespoons chocolate and hazelnut spread, then top with the bananas and ice cream.

cherry & coconut sponge pudding

Preparation time **15 minutes**
Cooking temperature **high**
Cooking time **3–3½ hours**
Serves **4–6**

butter, for greasing
40 g (1½ oz) **desiccated
  coconut**
400 g (13 oz) can **cherry pie
  filling**
500 g (1 lb) pack **Madeira
  cake mix**
4 tablespoons **sunflower oil**
  or **1 egg** (see cake mix
  instructions)

Preheat the slow cooker if necessary; see the
manufacturer's instructions. Lightly butter a 1.5 litre
(2½ pint) pudding basin and base-line with a circle of
nonstick baking paper, checking first it will fit in the slow
cooker pot. Sprinkle in a little of the coconut, then tilt and
turn the basin until the buttery sides are lightly coated.
Spoon half the cherry pie filling into the base of the basin.

Tip the cake mix into a bowl and mix in the oil or egg and
water according to the pack instructions. Stir in the
remaining coconut, then spoon the mixture into the basin
and spread it level. Cover the top with buttered, domed
foil and lower the basin into the slow cooker pot.

Pour boiling water into the slow cooker pot to come
halfway up the sides of the basin. Cover with the lid and
cook on high for 3–3½ hours or until the sponge is well
risen, feels dry and springs back when pressed with a
fingertip.

Lift the basin out of the slow cooker pot using a tea
towel and remove the foil. Loosen the edge of the
pudding with a knife, turn out on to a plate and peel off
the lining paper. Heat the remaining pie filling in a small
saucepan or the microwave until hot. Serve the pudding
in bowls with the warm cherries and scoops of vanilla
ice cream, if liked.

For spiced chocolate cherry sponge pudding, line
the pudding basin with cherry pie filling as above,
omitting the coconut. Make up a 500 g (1 lb)
chocolate-flavoured Madeira cake mix with 1 teaspoon
ground cinnamon and the sunflower oil or egg and
continue as above.

206

raspberry & rhubarb oaty crumble

Preparation time **15 minutes**
Cooking temperature **low**
Cooking time **2–3 hours**
Serves **4**

400 g (13 oz) trimmed
 rhubarb
150 g (5 oz) frozen
 raspberries
50 g (2 oz) **caster sugar**
3 tablespoons **water**

Topping
15 g (½ oz) **butter**
3 tablespoons **flaked**
 almonds
200 g (7 oz), **ready-made**
 flapjacks (about 4)

Preheat the slow cooker if necessary; see the manufacturer's instructions. Cut the rhubarb into 2.5 cm (1 inch) thick slices and add to the slow cooker pot with the still-frozen raspberries, the sugar and water. Cover with the lid and cook on low for 2–3 hours or until the rhubarb is just tender.

When almost ready to serve, heat the butter in a frying pan, add the almonds and crumble in the flapjacks. Fry, stirring, for 3–4 minutes or until hot and lightly browned. Spoon the fruit into bowls, sprinkle the crumble over the top and serve with thick cream.

For peach & mixed berry crumble, dice 3 fresh peaches, discarding the stones, and add to the slow cooker pot with 150 g (5 oz) mixed still-frozen summer fruits, the sugar and water. Cook and sprinkle with the flapjack topping as above.

chocolate croissant pudding

Preparation time **15 minutes**
Cooking temperature **low**
Cooking time **4–4½ hours**
Serves **4**

50 g (2 oz) **butter**
4 **chocolate croissants**
50 g (2 oz) **caster sugar**
¼ teaspoon **ground cinnamon**
40 g (1½ oz) **pecan nuts**,
   roughly crushed
300 ml (½ pint) **milk**
2 **eggs**
2 **egg yolks**
1 teaspoon **vanilla extract**

Butter the inside of a 1.2 litre (2 pint) straight-sided heatproof dish with a little of the butter, checking first that it will fit into the slow cooker pot.

Slice the croissants thickly and spread one side of each slice with the remaining butter. Mix together the sugar and spice. Arrange the croissants in layers in the dish, sprinkling each layer with the spiced sugar and the pecans.

Whisk the milk, whole eggs, egg yolks and vanilla extract in a bowl. Pour into the dish and leave to soak for 15 minutes. Preheat the slow cooker if necessary; see the manufacturer's instructions.

Cover the top of the dish loosely with buttered foil and lower it into the slow cooker pot. Pour boiling water into the pot to come halfway up the sides of the dish, cover with the lid and cook on low for 4–4½ hours or until the custard is set and the pudding well risen. Lift the dish out of the slow cooker pot using a tea towel. Dust with sifted icing sugar. Scoop into bowls and serve with cream.

For bread & butter pudding, spread 40 g (1½ oz) butter over 4 thick slices of bread, cut into triangles and layer in the buttered dish with 3 tablespoons luxury mixed dried fruit and the sugar. Pour the custard over the bread and continue as above.

drinks & preserves

beetroot chutney

Preparation time **30 minutes**
Cooking temperature **high**
Cooking time **6–7 hours**
Makes **4** jars of assorted sizes

1 bunch of raw **beetroot**,
   about 5 in total, trimmed and
   peeled
500 g (1 lb) **red plums**,
   stoned and roughly chopped
1 large **onion**, finely chopped
250 ml (8 fl oz) **red wine**
   vinegar
250 g (8 oz) **light muscovado**
   sugar
4 cm (1½ inches) **fresh root**
   ginger, peeled and finely
   chopped
1 tablespoon **star anise**
   pieces, crushed
1 teaspoon **peppercorns**,
   crushed
1 teaspoon **ground cinnamon**

Preheat the slow cooker if necessary; see the manufacturer's instructions. Coarsely grate the beetroot and put it into the slow cooker pot with all the remaining ingredients.

Mix everything together thoroughly, then cover with the lid and cook on high for 6–7 hours, stirring once or twice, until the beetroot is tender and the plums pulpy.

Warm 4 clean jars in a low oven for 5 minutes. Ladle the hot chutney into the warm jars, cover the surface with waxed discs and screw the lids in place. Label and store in a cool place until required. Once opened, store in the refrigerator.

Serve with cheese, cold sliced ham or with the Courgette & Broad Bean Frittata (see pages 66–67).

For chillied beetroot & tomato chutney, make up the chutney as the recipe above, replacing the plums with 500 g (1 lb) diced tomatoes and the ginger and spices with 1 teaspoon smoked paprika, 1 teaspoon crushed dried red chillies, 1 teaspoon ground cinnamon, ½ teaspoon ground allspice and salt and pepper.

apple, thyme & rosemary jelly

Preparation time **40 minutes**
Cooking temperature **high**
Cooking time **2–3 hours**
Makes **3** jars of assorted sizes

1 kg (2 lb) **cooking apples**
(not peeled or cored),
washed and diced
125 ml (4 fl oz) **red wine** or
cider vinegar
600 ml (1 pint) boiling **water**
about 625 g (1¼ lb)
granulated sugar
1 tablespoon **thyme leaves**,
stripped from the stems
2 tablespoons finely chopped
rosemary leaves

Preheat the slow cooker if necessary; see the manufacturer's instructions. Put the apples and vinegar into the slow cooker pot and pour over the boiling water. Cover with the lid and cook on high for 2–3 hours or until the apples are tender. Don't worry if the apples discolour.

Hang a jelly bag from a frame or upturned stool and set a bowl beneath it. Ladle the cooked apples and their juices into the bag and allow to drip through.

Measure the liquid and pour it into a large saucepan; for every 600 ml (1 pint) liquid add 500 g (1 lb) of sugar. Heat gently, stirring occasionally, until the sugar has dissolved, then boil rapidly for about 15 minutes until setting point is reached. Check with a jam thermometer or spoon a little of the jelly on to a saucer that has been chilled in the refrigerator. Leave for 1–2 minutes, then run a finger through the jelly. If a finger space is left and the jelly has wrinkled it is ready; if not boil for 5–10 minutes more and then retest.

Skim any scum with a slotted spoon, then stir in the chopped herbs. Leave the jelly to stand for 5 minutes.

Warm 3 clean jars in a low oven for 5 minutes. Ladle the jelly into the warm jars, cover the surface with waxed discs, add cellophane jam pot covers and secure with elastic bands. Label and store in a cool place. Once opened, store in the refrigerator. Serve with lamb.

For apple & blackberry jelly, put 750 g (1½ lb) cooking apples, washed and diced, into the slow cooker pot with 250 g (8 oz) blackberries, 125 ml (4 fl oz) lemon juice and the boiling water. Continue as above, omitting the herbs. Serve with scones.

orange marmalade

Preparation time **45 minutes**,
plus overnight cooling
Cooking temperature **low**
Cooking time **8–10 hours**
Makes **6** jars of assorted sizes

1 kg (2 lb) **Seville oranges**
1.2 litres (2 pints) boiling
water
2 kg (4 lb) **preserving** or
granulated sugar

Preheat the slow cooker if necessary; see the manufacturer's instructions. Put the whole oranges into the slow cooker pot, cover with the boiling water and put an upturned saucer on top of the oranges to stop them from floating.

Cover with the lid and cook on low for 8–10 hours or until the oranges are tender. Lift the pot out of the housing using oven gloves and leave to cool overnight. The next day, lift the oranges out of the slow cooker pot, draining well. Cut into quarters, scoop out and discard the pips, then thinly slice the oranges.

Put the sliced oranges and the liquid from the slow cooker pot into a preserving pan or large saucepan, add the sugar and heat gently, stirring occasionally until the sugar has completely dissolved. Increase the heat, and boil for 20–30 minutes or until setting point is reached (see page 216).

Warm 6 clean jars in a low oven for 5 minutes. Ladle the hot marmalade into the warm jars, cover the surface with waxed discs, add cellophane jam pot covers and secure with elastic bands or screw the jar lids in place. Label and store in a cool place until required.

For dark ginger orange marmalade, cook the Seville oranges with 75 g (3 oz) peeled and finely chopped fresh root ginger in the slow cooker as above. Make up the marmalade with the sliced oranges and ginger as above, using 1.5 kg (3½ lb) preserving or granulated sugar and 500 g (1 lb) light muscovado sugar.

passion fruit & lime curd

Preparation time **15 minutes**
Cooking temperature **low**
Cooking time **3–4 hours**
Makes **3** small jars

125 g (4 oz) **unsalted butter,**
   diced
400 g (13 oz) **caster sugar**
4 **eggs**, beaten
grated rind and juice of
   2 **limes**
grated rind of 2 **lemons**
juice of 1 **lemon**
3 **passion fruit**, halved

Preheat the slow cooker if necessary; see the manufacturer's instructions. Put the butter and sugar in a large basin, checking first that it will fit into the slow cooker pot, then heat in the microwave until the butter has just melted. Alternatively, heat the butter and sugar in a saucepan and pour into the basin.

Stir the sugar mix, then gradually whisk in the eggs, and then the fruit rind and juice. Cover the basin with foil and lower into the slow cooker pot. Pour boiling water into the pot to come halfway up the sides of the basin. Cover with the lid and cook on low for 3–4 hours, stirring once during cooking, until thick.

Stir once more, then scoop the passion fruit seeds out of the halved fruit with a teaspoon and stir them into the preserve.

Warm 3 clean jars in a low oven for 5 minutes. Ladle the preserve into the warm jars, cover the surface with waxed discs, add cellophane jam pot covers and secure with elastic bands or screw the lids in place. Label and leave to cool. The preserve can be stored for up to 2 weeks in the refrigerator.

For lemon curd, make up as above, using the rind and juice of 3 lemons and omitting the lime rind and juice and passion fruit.

apricot conserve

Preparation time **15 minutes**
Cooking temperature **high**
Cooking time **3–5 hours**
Makes **3** jars of assorted sizes

300 g (10 oz) ready-to-eat
    dried **apricots**, diced
4 **peaches**, halved, stoned
    and diced
250 g (8 oz) **caster sugar**
300 ml (½ pint) boiling **water**

Preheat the slow cooker if necessary; see the manufacturer's instructions. Put the apricots, peaches, sugar and boiling water into the slow cooker pot and stir together.

Cover with the lid and cook on high for 3–5 hours, stirring once during cooking and then again at the end, until the fruit is soft and the liquid thick and syrupy, with a texture like chutney.

Warm 3 clean jars in a low oven for 5 minutes. Ladle the conserve into the warm jars. Cover the surface with waxed discs, add cellophane jam pot covers and secure with elastic bands or screw the jar lids in place. Label and leave to cool. The conserve can be stored for up to 2 months in the refrigerator.

For apricot & orange conserve, put 400 g (13 oz) dried apricots, the grated rind and juice of 1 large orange, the sugar and the boiling water in the slow cooker pot, omitting the peaches. Continue as above.

hot spiced berry punch

Preparation time **10 minutes**
Cooking temperature **high** and
 low
Cooking time **3–4 hours**
Serves **6**

1 litre (1¾ pints) **cranberry
 and raspberry drink**
250 g (8 oz) frozen **berry
 fruits**
50 g (2 oz) **caster sugar**
4 tablespoons **crème de
 cassis** (optional)
4 small **star anise**
1 **cinnamon stick**, halved
 lengthways
fresh **raspberries**, to decorate
 (optional)

Preheat the slow cooker if necessary; see the manufacturer's instructions. Pour the cranberry and raspberry drink into the slow cooker pot. Add the frozen fruits, the sugar and crème de cassis, if using. Stir together, then add the star anise and halved cinnamon stick.

Cover with the lid and cook on high for 1 hour. Reduce the heat and cook on low for 2–3 hours, or set to auto for 3–4 hours, until piping hot.

Strain, if liked, then put the star anise and cinnamon into small heatproof glasses. Ladle the hot punch into the glasses and add a few fresh raspberries, if liked.

For boozy berry punch, replace the crème de cassis with 150 ml (¼ pint) vodka and make up the recipe as above.

For spiced berry and pear compote, make up the punch as above. Peel, core and slice 4 ripe pears and arrange in a heatproof serving dish. Pour over 300 ml (½ pint) of the hot punch and allow to cool. Serve as a dessert or breakfast accompaniment topped with spoonfuls of Greek yogurt flavoured with a little honey. Serve the remaining hot punch in glasses as above.

cider toddy

Preparation time **10 minutes**

Cooking temperature **high** and **low**

Cooking time **3–4 hours**

Serves **6**

1 litre (1¾ pints) **dry cider**
125 ml (4 fl oz) **whisky**
125 ml (4 fl oz) **orange juice**
4 tablespoons **set honey**
2 **cinnamon sticks**
orange wedges and **curls**, to decorate (optional)

Preheat the slow cooker if necessary; see the manufacturer's instructions. Add all the ingredients to the slow cooker pot, cover with the lid and cook on high for 1 hour.

Reduce the heat and cook on low for 2–3 hours, or set to auto for 3–4 hours, until piping hot. Stir, then ladle into heatproof tumblers. Add orange wedges and curls to decorate, if liked.

For gingered cider toddy, replace the whisky with 125 ml (4 fl oz) ginger wine and 2 tablespoons finely chopped stem ginger and make up the recipe as above.

For citrus toddy, pour 150 ml (¼ pint) whisky into the slow cooker pot, add 125 g (4 oz) set honey, 100 g (3½ oz) caster sugar and 750 ml (1¼ pints) cold water, then add the grated rind of 1 orange, the juice of 3 oranges, the grated rind of 1 lemon and the juice of 3 lemons. Roughly crush 8 cardamom pods, add the pods and seeds to the slow cooker pot. Cover and cook as above.

mulled wine

Preparation time **5 minutes**
Cooking temperature **high** and
  low
Cooking time **3–4 hours**
Serves **6**

750 ml (1¼ pints) or 1 bottle
  inexpensive **red wine**
300 ml (½ pint) **clear apple
  juice**
300 ml (½ pint) **water**
juice of 1 **orange**
1 **orange**, sliced
½ **lemon**, sliced
1 **cinnamon stick**, halved
6 **cloves**
2 **bay leaves**
125 g (4 oz) **caster sugar**
150 ml (1¼ pint) **brandy**

Preheat the slow cooker if necessary; see the manufacturer's instructions. Pour the wine, apple juice, water and orange juice into the slow cooker pot.

Add the sliced orange and lemon, the cinnamon stick, cloves and bay leaves, then mix in the sugar and brandy.

Cover with the lid and cook on high for 1 hour. Reduce the heat and cook on low for 2–3 hours, or set to auto for 3–4 hours, until piping hot. Ladle into heatproof glasses.

For cranberry mulled wine, replace the apple juice with 300 ml (½ pint) cranberry juice and 125 g (4 oz) fresh cranberries and make up the recipe as above.

For mulled wine jelly, cook the mulled wine as above. Spoon 6 tablespoons cold water into a bowl, sprinkle over 30 g (1 oz) gelatine, leave to soak for 5 minutes. Strain the mulled wine, stir in the gelatine until dissolved, then cool. Pour into 8 wine glasses and chill in the fridge until set. Top each of the mulled wine jellies with whipped cream.

hot buttered rum

Preparation time **5 minutes**
Cooking temperature **high** and
  low
Cooking time **3–4 hours**
Serves **6**

1 litre (1¾ pints) **clear apple
  juice**
150 ml (¼ pint) **dark rum**
2 tablespoons **set honey**
2 tablespoons **dark
  muscovado sugar**
25 g (1 oz) **butter**
6 **cloves**
1 **dessert apple**, cored and
  thickly sliced, to decorate

Preheat the slow cooker if necessary; see the
manufacturer's instructions. Put the apple juice, rum,
honey, sugar, butter and cloves into the slow cooker
pot.

Cover with the lid and cook on high for 1 hour. Reduce
the heat and cook on low for 2–3 hours, or set to auto
for 3–4 hours, until piping hot.

Stir, scoop out the cloves, then ladle the punch into
heatproof tumblers. Decorate with slices of apple.

For hot buttered calvados, replace the rum with
150 ml (¼ pint) calvados (apple brandy) and make
up the recipe as above.

For poached apples with buttered rum, once the
punch is made pour into a serving jug keeping 300 ml
(½ pint) in the slow cooker pot. Add 4 medium-sized
cooking apples that have been quartered, cored and
peeled, cover and cook on high for 1–1½ hours until
the apples are tender. Serve as a dessert with scoops
of vanilla ice cream.

skier's hot chocolate

Preparation time **10 minutes**
Cooking temperature **low**
Cooking time **2–3 hours**
Serves **4**

100 g (3½ oz) good-quality
  chocolate
25 g (1 oz) **caster sugar**
750 ml (1¼ pints) full-fat **milk**
few drops of **vanilla extract**
little **ground cinnamon**
3 tablespoons **Kahlúa coffee
  liqueur** (optional)
mini marshmallows, to serve

Preheat the slow cooker if necessary; see the manufacturer's instructions. Put the chocolate and sugar in the slow cooker pot, then add the milk, vanilla extract and cinnamon.

Cover with the lid and cook on low for 2–3 hours, whisking once or twice, until the chocolate has melted and the drink is hot. Stir in the Kahlúa, if using. Ladle into mugs and top with a few mini marshmallows.

For hot chocolate with brandy cream, make up the hot chocolate as above, replacing the Kahlua with 3 tablespoons brandy. Whip 125 ml (4 fl oz) double cream with 2 tablespoons of icing sugar until soft peaks form, then gradually whisk in 3 tablespoons brandy. Pour the hot chocolate into mugs, then top with spoonfuls of the whipped cream and dust lightly with drinking chocolate powder or grated chocolate.

For Mexican hot chocolate, put 50 g (2 oz) cocoa and 4 teaspoons instant coffee into the slow cooker pot. Measure 1 litre (1¾ pint) of boiling water. Make a smooth paste by mixing a little of the boiling water with the cocoa and coffee. Add the rest of the water, 150 ml (¼ pint) rum, 100 g (3½ oz) caster sugar, ½ teaspoon ground cinnamon and 1 dried red chilli, cut in half. Cover and cook on low for 3–4 hours. Discard the chilli and ladle into 4 cups. Top with 150 ml (¼ pint) double cream.

index

acknowledgements

Executive Editor: Eleanor Maxfield
Managing Editor: Clare Churly
Deputy Art Director: Yasia Williams
Designer: Penny Stock
Photographer: Stephen Conroy
Home Economist: Sara Lewis
Props Stylist: Liz Hippisley
Senior Production Controller: Caroline Alberti

We would like to thank **Morphy Richards** for the kind
loan of their slow cookers for recipe testing.

Special photography: © Octopus Publishing Group
Limited/Stephen Conroy